THE UNIVERSITY OF MICHIGAN
CENTER FOR CHINESE STUDIES

MICHIGAN PAPERS IN CHINESE STUDIES
NO. 24

CHINESE COMMUNIST MATERIALS AT THE BUREAU OF INVESTIGATION ARCHIVES, TAIWAN

by

Peter Donovan, Carl E. Dorris,
and Lawrence R. Sullivan

Ann Arbor

Center for Chinese Studies
The University of Michigan

1976

CONTENTS

vi

ACKNOWLEDGMENTS

Research on this project was carried out at the Bureau of Investigation, Taipei, Taiwan, Republic of China, from August 1973 to January 1974. We would like to thank Mr. Ch'en Sen-wen, chief of the Documents Section, and his staff for their cooperation. We would also like to express our gratitude to Knight Biggerstaff, Y. C. Chang, Albert Feuerwerker, Richard Howard, John Israel, Michel Oksenberg, Richard Solomon, and P. K. Yu for their criticisms of earlier drafts of this survey. Special thanks is given to Harriet Mills and Wan Wei-ying for their painstaking help in documentary translations and to John Ma who suggested this project. In addition, we must thank the Center for Chinese Studies, The University of Michigan, for its financial support towards the preparation of this manuscript, Andrea Morgan, Jeannie Lin, and Gay McDonald for their editing and excellent typing, and Dorothy Perng for her calligraphy.

Finally, we owe a debt of gratitude to the Fulbright-Hays Fellowship Program and the Foreign Area Fellowship Program for supporting the dissertation research in Taiwan from which this survey was drawn.

Peter Donovan
Carl E. Dorris
Lawrence R. Sullivan

LIST OF ABBREVIATIONS

BIC	Bureau of Investigation Collection
CC	Central Committee
CCP	Chinese Communist Party
CCPCC	Chinese Communist Party Central Committee
CPSU	Communist Party of the Soviet Union
GYL	Communist Youth League
KMT	Kuomintang

INTRODUCTION

During the long years of civil strife in China the Nationalist authorities amassed extensive materials on their Communist adversaries. Now stored in government institutions on Taiwan these materials are an excellent source for the study of the Chinese Communist movement. Two collections open for research are especially important. One is the Bureau of Intelligence, Ministry of Defense, in Shih-lin, Taipei City, which provides good documentation on military history and, more generally, on all Chinese Communist affairs after 1949.[1] The other is the Bureau of Investigation Collection (BIC), Ministry of Justice, Hsin-tien, Taipei County.[2]

The BIC holds over 300,000 volumes of primary documents on the Chinese Communist movement.[3] The most valuable materials in this collection date from before 1949. Some were supplied by Nationalist agents or Communist defectors. Others were seized in the arrest of Communist cadres and the exposure of their political organizations. Still others were captured during periods of great turmoil, such as the destruction of the Chinese Communist Party (CCP) organization in China's cities from 1927 to 1933 and the fall of Kalgan to the Nationalist armies in 1947.[4] These documents, many of them originally secret, and generally unavailable in libraries and archives outside the People's Republic of China, constitute the core of the Bureau's collection. Materials from after 1949 are far fewer in number and reflect the Bureau's limited access to mainland sources. Of course, many of the documents in the BIC are also available elsewhere. For example, writings by Mao Tse-tung and most of the materials published on the mainland after 1949 are not unique to this collection. In addition, a set of microfilms marketed in Japan under the title <u>Materials on the Chinese Communist Party</u> appears to have been copied directly--and surreptitiously--from the BIC. The documents in this set date mainly from the War of Resistance (1937-1945) but also include Central Committee documents from 1932-1933.[5]

While the Bureau admits outside scholars, it uses these materials on the Communist movement primarily for its own research and publications.[6] Visitors may gain access to the archives by presenting letters of introduction from Chinese or foreign institutions, preferably through the Institute of International Relations.[7] The Bureau's wealth of materials has already attracted many scholars studying the Chinese Communist movement, and a number of important works have drawn

1

substantially on the BIC. Among them are: Hsiao Tso-liang, Power Relations Within the Chinese Communist Movement, 1931-1934; Ts'ao Po-i, The Rise and Fall of the Kiangsi Soviet (Chiang-hsi Su-wei-ai chih chien-li chi ch'i peng-k'uei); Mark Selden, The Yenan Way in Revolutionary China; John Israel, Student Nationalism in China: 1927-1937; Tetsuya Kataoka, Resistance and Revolution in China; Roy Hofheinz, "Peasant Movements and Rural Revolution: Chinese Communism in the Countryside, 1923-1927"; and Lyman Van Slyke, Enemies and Friends: The United Front in Chinese Communist History. [8]

Certain aspects of the Chinese Communist movement are particularly well documented in BIC materials, and these are stressed in this survey of the collection. [9] Almost every level of the Chinese Communist Party and affiliated organizations as well as every kind of document are represented in the BIC; included are internal communications as well as published books, periodicals, posters, letters, and handbills from the Central Committee and from provincial, county, and city and district committees, from local branches, and from many special units of the CCP. [10]

By period, the BIC's greatest strength lies in documents from 1927 to 1949. There are some earlier materials, but the 1921-1927 period of CCP history is better documented in the Kuomintang archives in Ch'ing-t'an, Taipei County. [11] The late 1920s and early 1930s are very well documented in the BIC. However, much of the material from the Kiangsi Soviet (1931-1934) is not catalogued by the Bureau and consequently difficult to obtain. Moreover, we do not know the extent of overlap between the BIC's material on the Kiangsi Soviet and the independent Ch'en Ch'eng Collection, which is widely available on microfilm. [12] The War of Resistance (1937-1945) is probably the best documented period in the collection. The Civil War (1946-1949) is also well covered.

Geographically, the majority of BIC documents come from the Party's major base areas at any time: Shanghai in the late 1920s and early 1930s, the Kiangsi Soviet from 1931 to 1934, and the North China base areas after 1937. Also represented are secondary areas of operation such as those in Manchuria, Hopeh, Anhwei, Chekiang, and the O-Yü-Wan Soviet during the early 1930s; Central China during the War of Resistance and Civil War periods; and Hainan Island during the Civil War and post-Liberation periods. [13] In addition, the BIC has numerous reports and analyses on the CCP made by agencies of the Nationalist government. [14]

There are problems in using the BIC, the most serious of which is the absence of any comprehensive guide to the collection. Tokuda Noriyuki's "Guide to Materials Relating to the History of the Chinese Communist Party" lists many documents in the BIC, organizing them under such headings as "politics" and "the united front."[15] Available on Taiwan is a union catalogue of materials on the Communist movement, which lists the holdings of nine different libraries there, including the BIC.[16] The Bureau's own card catalogue is roughly organized by a decimal system peculiar to government institutions on Taiwan. Works on the Chinese Communist movement fall mainly under "periodicals," "the Chinese Communist Party," "the Communist International," and "social sciences." But within these categories there is no particular order by title or author, either by phonetic system or stroke order. Cards give title, author, publisher, and place and date of publication where the information can be easily determined from the documents, but most cards are incomplete. In addition, the card catalogue fails to list all the BIC's holdings. Indeed, it does not list many important documents from the Central Committee in the early 1930s and omits all of its newspapers. Unfortunately, as the user must call for books and may not enter the stacks, he is forced to rely on the card catalogue.

Another serious problem is the condition of the documents. Some are yellowed and crumbling, and on others the characters have faded. Some are printed or mimeographed from handwriting; yet others are original handwritten documents, often in almost indecipherable cursive script.[17] Some documents are damaged. All have been bound.

Our purpose in this survey is, without any attempt at a comprehensive listing of the Bureau's holdings, to give scholars a representative description of the collection. Also, we shall point out its implications for research on some of the important issues in the history of the Chinese Communist movement and suggest new areas for research at the Bureau in the fields of political science and history.

FOOTNOTES TO INTRODUCTION

1. For a description of materials in the Bureau of Intelligence, see Appendix A.

2. Tiao-ch'a-chü, Ssu-fa-pu, Hsin-tien, T'ai-pei hsien (調查局 , 司法部 ， 新店 ， 臺北縣).

3. A Brief Introduction of the Library (Tzu-liao chien-chieh 資料簡介), (Hsin-tien, Taipei: The Research Institute and Library, Investigation Bureau, Ministry of Justice, no date). According to the staff, all the documents on file are from the Bureau's original central headquarters in Nanking.

4. Peter J. Seybolt's brief but useful guide to research on the CCP discusses the BIC. See Peter J. Seybolt, The Chinese Communist Movement 1921-1949; Sources and Perspectives, paper delivered at a meeting of the Association for Asian Studies, 1972.

5. Materials on the Chinese Communist Party (Yūkan Chūgoku Kyōsanto shiryō 有關中國共產黨資料), (Tokyo: Yushodo Film Publications, Ltd.). Twenty reels of microfilm, 393 items. Yushodo published a checklist of the documents in this collection, and the Harvard-Yenching Library has compiled another list alphabetized by title (Wade-Giles system) with information on author, date of publication, etc. See Seybolt, p. 6.

6. For an example of a publication based on BIC documents, see, Wang Chang-ling (王章陵), History of the Chinese Communist Youth League (Chung-kuo kung-ch'an-chu-i ch'ing-nien-t'uan shih-lun 中國共產主義青年團史論), (Taipei: Institute of East Asian Studies, 1973).

7. For a description of materials available at the Institute of International Relations, see Appendix B.

8. Hsiao Tso-liang, Power Relations Within the Chinese Communist Movement, 1931-1934 (Seattle: University of Washington Press, 1961); Ts'ao Po-i, The Rise and Fall of the Kiangsi Soviet (Chiang-hsi Su-wei-ai chih chien-li chi ch'i peng-k'uei) (Taipei:

Institute of East Asian Studies, 1972); Mark Selden, <u>The Yenan Way in Revolutionary China</u> (Cambridge: Harvard University Press, 1971); John Israel, <u>Student Nationalism in China: 1927-1937</u> (Stanford: Hoover Institution, 1966); Tetsuya Kataoka, <u>Resistance and Revolution in China: The Communists and the Second United Front</u> (Berkeley: University of California Press, 1974); Roy Hofheinz, "Peasant Movements and Rural Revolution: Chinese Communism in the Countryside, 1923-1927" (Ph.D. Dissertation, Harvard, 1966); and Lyman Van Slyke, <u>Enemies and Friends: The United Front in Chinese Communist History</u> (Stanford: Stanford University Press, 1967).

9. Comparisons of the BIC with the major collections on the Chinese Communist movement in the United States are difficult and are not generally considered in this survey. However, in the case of the Hoover Institution on War, Peace, and Revolution a brief comparison is in order. Generally speaking, the post-1949 period of the People's Republic is best represented in the Hoover collection, although there are some valuable documents in the Bureau which we cite in this survey. On the other hand, the Bureau's documentation from the period of the late 1920s and the 1930s is superior to Hoover's, particularly those materials from the provincial and county levels of the CCP. Finally, coverage of the 1940s in the two collections is largely the same. But Hoover is more representative of the Shen-Kan-Ning Border Region and, more particularly, Yenan, while the BIC's strength lies in its documentation from other North China base areas, such as Chin-Ch'a-Chi and Chin-Chi-Lu-Yü.

10. For a special unit of the CCP, see <u>Chinese Soviet Republic, Political Security Bureau, Hsiang-O-Kan Provincial Bureau, Proclamation No. 2</u> (Chung-hua Su-wei-ai kung-ho-kuo cheng-chih pao-wei-chü, Hsiang-O-Kan sheng-fen-chü, pu-kao ti-erh hao 中華蘇維埃共和國政治保衛局, 湘鄂贛省分局佈告, 第二號), poster, no BIC number.

11. Examples of documents in the Kuomintang Party Archives on the CCP in the 1920s include: Yun Tai-ying (惲代英), <u>The Youth Movement in the Past Year</u> (I-nien-lai ti ch'ing-nien yun-tung 一年來的青年運動); T'an P'ing-shan (譚平山), <u>An Account of the Chinese Railway Workers' Strike Movement</u> (Chung-kuo t'ieh-lu kung-jen pa-kung yun-tung chi 中國鐵路工人

罷工運動記); and Chang T'e-li (張特立), pseudonym of Chang Kuo-t'ao (張國燾), A Brief History of the Trade Unions Movement Before and After the February Seventh Railway Strike (Erh-ch'i ch'ien-hou kung-hui yun-tung lueh-shih 二七前後工會運動略史).

12. Ch'en Ch'eng Collection (Shih-sou tzu-liao shih-pien 石叟 資料室編); an index of the Ch'en Ch'eng collection is available from the Hoover Institution. See An Index to Chinese Communist Materials in the Shih Sou Collection (Shih Sou tzu-liao shih kung-fei tzu-liao mu-lu 石叟資料室共匪 資料目錄).

While he was curator of the East Asian Collection of the Hoover Institution, Mr. Eugene Wu acquired this collection for in-house research. The Hoover Institution began the distribution of this set of 21 reels of microfilm after Mr. Wu's move to Harvard University.

13. For abbreviated place names used by the CCP, see, Geographical Terms, Glossary C.

14. The issuing authority of investigative reports by the Nationalist government are listed in the BIC card catalogue as "Central Investigation and Statistical Bureau [Office]" (Chung-yang tiao-ch'a t'ung chi-chü [shih] 中央調查統計局[室]), or Internal Security Investigation Bureau (Nei-cheng-pu-tiao-ch'a-chü 內政部調查局), or Unity Publishing House (T'ung-i ch'u-pan-she 統一出版社).

15. Tokuda Noriyuki, "Guide to Materials Relating to the History of the Chinese Communist Party," ("Chūkyō tō shi kankei shiryō mokuroku" 中共黨史關係資料目錄) Bulletin of the Center for Contemporary Chinese Studies (Kindai Chūgoku Kenkyu Senta I Ho 近代中國研究センター彙報), No. 9, (July 1967), pp. 8-20; No. 10 (October 1967), pp. 8-24. Unfortunately Tokuda does not give BIC call numbers so that when using the collection, one must look through the card catalogue-- a time consuming process--to find the numbers.

16. Communist Affairs Research Coordinating Center. Union Catalog of Chinese Language Materials on Communist Affairs (Fei-ch'ing

yen-chiu hsieh-t'iao chung-hsin chung-wen fei-ch'ing t'u-shu lien-
ho mu-lu 匪情研究協調中心中文匪情
圖書聯合目錄) (Mu-cha, Taipei: Institute of International Relations, 1962), 2 volumes; supplementary volume added
in 1966 and again in 1971. A copy is available at the Institute
of International Relations.

17. See, Reproduction Techniques, Glossary E.

I. PARTY AFFAIRS

Perhaps the major attraction of the BIC is the collection of documents on the structure and functioning of the Chinese Communist Party. These include unpublished reports, decisions, and communications from various levels of the Party's hierarchy in the periods 1928-1934 and 1937-1950. CCP materials are also available from the years of the First United Front (1922-1927) and from the interim period of the Long March and the establishment of the Resistance Base Areas (1934-1937), but only a scattered and limited selection.

A. The Period of the Soviets, 1927-1934

In the years after Chiang Kai-shek's destruction of the CCP in Shanghai and Canton in 1927, the Chinese Communists confronted a critical challenge to their ideological legitimacy and political survival. Following decisions from the Sixth Party Congress held in the Soviet Union (1928), a succession of Party leaders attempted to rebuild the shattered CCP apparatus in the cities.[1] Yet, as the prospects of an urban revolution in China diminished, the focus of Communist activities shifted to the rural Soviets established in Kiangsi and several other provinces.

Scholars interested in the last months of the First United Front and the subsequent effort of the leadership to rebuild the CCP, will find interesting, though limited, materials in the BIC. The Bureau holds two issues of a Shanghai District Party Magazine, published just before the Nationalist armies seized the city; a Central Committee report on the Canton Commune; and a CC resolution regarding propaganda and factionalism in the Party.[2] Other materials from this period--including a report of the Second Plenum of the Sixth Party Congress (1929),[3] minutes of an enlarged Politburo meeting in March 1930,[4] and the newspaper Red Flag Daily,[5]--document the attacks on Ch'en Tu-hsiu and Ch'ü Ch'iu-pai and trace the rise of Li Li-san. Of particular interest are a periodical, Shanghai Tide (Hu-ch'ao), issued under the auspices of Li's newly installed Party Secretariat (mi-shu-ch'u) in Shanghai and a letter from Ho Tzu-shu, a member of the Russian Returned Student faction assigned to the Shanghai Party Committee and one of the earliest opponents of Li.[6] Especially important are the Bureau's collections of the Central Correspondence (Chung-yang t'ung-hsin);[7] Central Circular (Chung-yang t'ung-kao);[8] and the Organization Bulletin (Tsu-chih t'ung-hsun).[9] These document the development of organization and of revolutionary strategies, and the policy conflicts that grew out of the Party's final attempts to seize control of China's cities in the late 1920s and early 1930s.[10]

Materials from the Party's center give an accurate account of its internal politics before 1937. Among Central Committee materials,[11] there is a particularly rich collection from 1932-1933.[12] This collection covers major policy decisions by the new leaders from the Russian Returned Students faction, as well as Central directives on such topics as branch work, internal security, and cadre work style. Other documents demonstrate the commitment of the Russian Returned Students to the eradication of the "Li Li-san Line" and to the further "Bolshevization" of the Party.[13] Finally, there is valuable material in the BIC bearing on purges of important Party leaders.[14]

Major publications of the CCP's Central Propaganda Bureau include Red Flag Weekly (Hung-ch'i chou-pao),[15] Party Construction (Tang ti chien-she),[16] and Struggle (Tou-cheng).[17] Struggle was devoted primarily to the Shanghai Party organization and details such little-known aspects of the CCP in the 1930s as factory branch organization and the occupational composition of the Shanghai Party membership.[18] Numerous issues of these periodicals can be acquired elsewhere, but the Bureau's collection appears to be more complete.

Many documents in the BIC cover the provincial level of the CCP's organization. The majority are from the Kiangsu Party Committee, which was located in Shanghai, and the remainder are from Party committees in Anhwei, Chekiang, Fukien, Hopei, Shensi, Shantung, and Manchuria.[19] Numbering over one hundred catalog entries, they treat in depth the involvement of provincial committees in disputes that affected the entire CCP during this volatile period of its history. Among the most interesting are a complete set of the journal Lenin Life (Lieh-ning sheng-huo) published by the Kiangsu Provincial Committee during the CCP's underground struggle in Shanghai;[20] scattered issues of Struggle and Study (Tou-cheng yü hsueh-hsi) from Shensi,[21] and the newspaper Fukien Red Flag (Fu-chien hung-ch'i).[22] In addition, special provincial reports, minutes of provincial Party meetings, and letters from provincial committees to cadres in the field and other CCP units are numerous and offer excellent sources for analyzing the diversity of CCP organization and practices below the central level.[23] The minutes of an Enlarged Executive Committee of the Fukien Party organization[24] and a document on criticism and self-criticism in the Shensi Provincial Committee[25] are particularly revealing in this respect.

At lower levels of the Party--county, city and district, and branch--there are similar but far fewer documents in the BIC.[26] There are some, though not many, documents from Party organizations in Shanghai, Tientsin, and Amoy,[27] and some--still fewer-- from CCP district organizations.[28] The most plentiful collection of materials from lower levels consist of documents from approximately fifty counties.[29] These include counties in Anhwei, Kiangsu, Fukien, Hupeh, and Kiangsi.[30] A particularly noteworthy document is Draft Resolutions of the First Enlarged Meeting of the Liu-an County Committee from Anhwei.[31]

The Bureau's holdings could also supplement research on the ideological struggle against various splinter groups within the CCP during the late 1920s and early 1930s. Some documents treat the Party's conflict in the early 1930s with the Trotskyites[32] and the Third Party. In addition, it would be interesting to look at the CCP from the vantage point of the KMT Left, as it appears in such publications as the Democratic Weekly (Min-chu chou-k'an).[33] Materials on these subjects, however, are widely available in the U.S. and Japan.

Documents from the CCP Soviets in the 1930s are not fully catalogued by the Bureau (as above) and are, consequently, difficult to assess. But discussions with the Bureau's staff and scholars familiar with the collection indicate that the BIC holds valuable material from the Central Kiangsi Soviet and from smaller rural soviets such as O-Yü-Wan,[34] Hsiang-O-hsi,[35] and O-hsi.[36] Some documents trace the establishment of the soviets in the early 1930s and treat the general problems of building a Communist Party organization in the countryside.[37] Others deal with specific policy decisions on land redistribution[38]--matters which are covered thoroughly in Hsiao Tso-liang's The Land Revolution in China.[39] There is valuable documentation from both local units of the Soviets[40] and the Central Soviet Organization,[41] including a detailed chart of Party and government institutions in the Central Soviet. Finally, decisions of the Party "Central" in Shanghai which express their policy views on the Soviets are available.[42]

12

B. The War of Resistance and the Civil War, 1937-1949

During the first two years of the war with Japan, the Chinese
Communist Party grew to tremendous size, but its development under
wartime conditions was uneven and the new membership included landlords and other "undesirables." In August 1939, the Central Committee issued an important directive on Party consolidation and initiated
a major internal reform and study drive. In conjunction with this
Party reform, the Central Committee began publication of the Communist (Kung-ch'an-tang jen) in September, which became the official
Party organ during the war.[43] Contributors included prominent
Central Party leaders such as Liu Shao-ch'i, Wang Chia-hsiang, Li
Fu-ch'un, Yang Sung, Li Wei-han, and Ai Ssu-ch'i. The Communist
reprinted all the major Central Committee directives and occasionally
offered local case studies of Party work. In the first issue the editors published the directive "On Party Consolidation" and devoted the
remainder of the edition to articles on various problems of internal
reform. In the same issue, Chang Wen-t'ien wrote on the rights
and responsibilities of Party members,[44] and an essay by Ch'en Yun
discussed Party consolidation and mass work in the war zones.[45]
The third issue examined the problems of recruiting intellectuals and
included an investigation report on Party branches in three villages of
Yen-ch'uan, Shensi.[46]

The Communist was the model for numerous other Party periodicals published at various regional and district committee levels. The
Shen-Kan-Ning Party Committee produced Unity (T'uan-chieh) from 1938
to 1943.[47] In North China there were a variety of internal Party
publications, among them the North China Bureau's Party Life (Tang
ti sheng-huo), the South Hopeh Committee's Plains (P'ing-yuan), and
the Chin-Chi-Yü Committee's War (Chan-tou). Unfortunately, the
Bureau has only single issues of two such periodicals, the Chin-Ch'a-
Chi Military District's New Great Wall (Hsin ch'ang-ch'eng) and the
Chi-Lu-Yü Committee's version of the Plains (P'ing-yuan).[48]

In wartime Party periodicals the BIC's strength is its holdings
from Central China. It has twenty-seven issues of Dawn (Fo-hsiao),
dating from April 1943 to July 1946.[49] The Huai-pei Su-Wan-Yü Committee edited Dawn and published a variety of local studies, reports
from other border area committees, and directives from the Central
China Bureau. The inaugural issue, for instance, reprinted Jen Pi-
shih's important report of January 1943 from the Northwest Bureau's

Senior Cadre Conference. Contributors in other issues were local
Party leaders such as Teng Tzu-hui, Liu Tzu-chiu, Feng Ting, and
P'eng Hsueh-feng. Dawn also has several excellent accounts of the
Rectification Drive (1942-1944) at the local level.

The BIC holds ten issues of Party Life (Tang ti sheng-huo), the
secret internal publication of the New Fourth Army's Chiang-pei Unit
Party Committee, which was located in the old O-Yü–Wan Soviet. 50
The committee's first edition is dated January 1941 and includes a
preface by the vice-commander of the New Fourth Army, Chang Yun-i.
Often, the editors of Party Life published directives from the Central
Committee and Central China Bureau as well as a number of local
Chiang-pei and O-Yü-Wan Committee circulars. These include articles
on the experiences and lessons of local Party work and essays promoting
the study of Marxism-Leninism. Most of these concern the Party's internal reform drive and study movement of 1939-1941, and the Rectification Drive of 1942 to 1944, with emphasis on strengthening Party
branch work and encouraging exemplary behavior by Party members.

Party Bulletin (Tang-nei t'ung-hsun), published by the Huai-pei
District Committee, concentrates on local affairs in Huai-pei from
1944 to 1945. The BIC has fifteen issues, with many articles written
by local cadres on village inspection work, the Great Production Drive
(1943-1946), rent and interest reduction, and branch reform. 51 There
are also scattered issues of several district committee magazines from
Central China such as Branch Bulletin (Chih-pu t'ung-hsun), Mass Bulletin (Ch'ün-chung t'ung-hsun), and War Life (Chan-tou sheng-huo). 52
Although there are only one or two issues of each, nonetheless, they
offer a variety of materials on local and community Party affairs.

The BIC has several issues of two of Central China's more
important internal Party magazines, the Central China Bureau's Central China Bulletin (Hua-chung t'ung-hsun) and the New Fourth Army
Seventh Division's Truth (Chen-li). 53 Two of the issues of Truth
deal with special topics. The August 1943 edition treats the experiences of cadres as they built base area in North China and includes
an important speech by P'eng Teh-huai. 54 The February 1944 issue
is on village investigation work in the Huai-pei region. In addition,
there are also several journals from the Huai-hai and Huai-nan Districts, the most important of which is the Huai-nan Party Magazine
(Huai-nan tang-k'an). 55

These journals constitute the BIC's richest source on Party affairs during the War of Resistance (1937-1945) and the Civil War (1946-1949). They discuss mass mobilization and the problems of internal Party reform at the time of the land reform movement of the late 1940s. Moreover, the articles emphasize the Rectification Drive and its impact on local party work and economic construction at the community level.

C. The Rectification Drive, 1942-1944

Students of Chinese Communist affairs have viewed the Rectification Drive from several perspectives. Some see it as essentially an educational movement aimed at indoctrinating cadres and Party members with a more distinctly Chinese version of Marxism-Leninism.[56] Others suggest that it was a power struggle between Mao Tse-tung and the Russian Returned Students over crucial policy questions.[57] Yet others argue that it was primarily a crystallization of wartime experiences into the mass line.[58] The BIC materials on rectification provide some new sources from which to reevaluate these interpretations.

Perhaps the most valuable documents come from the Northwest Bureau Senior Cadre Conference (October 1942 to January 1943). Following the six-month Rectification Study Movement in Yenan, this conference instituted a shift from study to internal Party reform and it redefined leadership style and economic goals. The BIC holds six of the major speeches given at the conference and the Northwest Bureau's summary of Conference activities. Among them are reports by Lin Po-ch'ü, Ho Lung, Kao Kang, and Jen Pi-shih, as well as the complete text of Mao Tse-tung's Economic Problems and Financial Problems--a summary of economic construction activities in the Shen-Kan-Ning Border Region, which first appeared in the 1947 version of Mao's Selected Works, published by the Chin-Ch'a-Chî Committee.[59]

A second group of documents includes various rectification and study materials from Communist base areas. For example, the Bureau has three volumes of a ten-volume set of rectification documents published by the Central Kiangsu Committee.[60] This committee compiled a number of essays and reports from regional leaders such as Jao Shu-shih. Also available in the BIC is the Chi-Lu-Yü Administrative Office's similar two-volume set, which published a wide variety of speeches and reports of second-line Party leaders whose works had not been included in the well-known twenty-two study documents used in the Rectification Study Movement and authorized by the Central Committee Propaganda Bureau.[61] Among them is an unusual collection of documents with three essays by Chang Wen-t'ien, who studied in the Soviet Union and is identified with the Russian Returned Students faction.[62]

A third group of rectification materials includes a number of district and county committee documents. For example, the Sixth District Committee Propaganda Bureau in the Chi-Lu-Yü Border Region printed a mimeographed volume for the study movement with local directives on how to initiate a study drive and issue an official study plan.[63] The Sixth District Committee also offered as reference materials a summary of the Shen-Kan-Ning experience and two excerpts from speeches by Chu Jui and Huang Ching on developing study and the nature of study itself.[64] There are also materials from the county level and notes made by individual Party members on their own experiences in the Rectification Drive.[65]

Finally, the BIC has the standard sources on rectification[66] as well as several studies of the movement by Nationalist intelligence analysts.[67] As for the rectification of Communist literature and propaganda, the BIC has only those documents commonly available in the West, such as Mao Tse-tung's speech at the Yenan Forum on Literature and Art[68] and a re-publication of Wang Shih-wei's The Wild Lily (Yeh pai-ho hua).[69] In addition, there are two little known Communist critiques of Wang, one by Chou Yang and another a collection of articles by Fan Wen-lan, Ai Ch'ing, and others.[70] There are also Nationalist intelligence reports on the literary "purge" carried out by the CCP following Mao's speech, but these add little to the detailed information on the Wang Shih-wei case found in issues of the Liberation Daily (Chieh-fang jih-pao).[71]

D. The Period of the People's Republic, 1949-1973

The BIC's holdings of post-1949 materials are understandably scarce, though there are some interesting exceptions. The collection of documents from the period immediately following the victory of the Communist Army includes original materials on cadre training and political study used by central, provincial, and local Party organs. From the Central Committee's Southern Bureau, for example, the BIC has several Communist Party Member Textbooks,[72] and from the Liao-yang City Party Committee there are numerous Political Study Reference Materials.[73] In some materials, such as How to Carry Out Theoretical Study from Shanghai[74] and Lectures on Basic Knowledge for Chinese Communist Party Members from the Wuhan Marxism-Leninism School,[75] the importance of the cadre's theoretical education emerges, while in others there is considerable discussion of "study" (hsueh-hsi) during both the Civil War and post-Liberation periods.[76] From provincial, county, and city Party committees there are handbooks and texts which describe propaganda work beginning in the late 1930s and extending through the early 1950s.[77] How to be a Propaganda Worker and several Propaganda Handbooks from Shanghai are particularly interesting and voluminous collections.[78]

In addition to the documentation covering the Party's actions on the mainland in the early 1950s, there are also limited materials regarding CCP activity on Chinese islands. For example, a publication from Canton treats CCP operations on Hainan island[79] and an investigation report conducted by the Bureau evaluates Communist organization on Taiwan up to 1950.[80]

Finally, the BIC holds other documents collected from the mainland by the Nationalist authorities since the early 1950s. These include public newspapers and internal Party materials, but their exclusion from the Bureau's card catalogue makes the scope of these materials difficult to assess. The newspapers are local, coming from cities and provinces, among them: The Shanghai Evening News (1966), Yin-ch'uan Daily (Szechwan, 1958), Ch'engtu Daily (1958), Pao-t'ou Daily (Inner Mongolia, 1957), Sian Daily (1958), Nanking Daily (1956-1957), Harbin Daily (1957), Yunnan Daily (1956-1957, 1972), Sinkiang Daily (1957), Inner Mongolian Daily (1958), and even some Mongolian-language newspapers.[81] Although we do not know the number of issues of each newspaper now available at the Bureau, these holdings appear limited, and only marginally important to research, especially for the period after 1953.

Classified CCP documents come from the Party's highest levels and seem to be of considerable importance. These include Mao Tse-tung's Highest-level Directives on the "rural rustification" (hsia-fang) of the Red Guards,[82] a cadre newspaper entitled Reference News,[83] and the "absolutely secret" Documents of the Chinese Communist Party Central Committee (1972),[84] one of which treats the Lin Piao affair. There is also the Political Work Bulletin from the 1970s which focuses on local problems, such as agricultural mechanization in a Kwangsi district and cultural works in a Pao-shan, Yunnan production team.[85]

FOOTNOTES TO CHAPTER I

1. For a discussion of the Sixth Party Congress by Ch'ü Ch'iu-pai (pseudonym Chih-fu), see Chih-fu (之 夫), [Conclusions of the Political Discussion at the Third Enlarged Plenum] Document Number Twelve of the Materials of the Third Plenum (San chung ch'üan-hui ts'ai-liao ti-shih-erh hao 三 中 全 會 材 料 第 十 二 號), September 1930, no BIC number.

2. Shanghai District Committee, Education Magazine (Chiao-yü tsa-chih 教 育 雜 誌), 1927, 052.1/814/9391; CCPCC, The Significance and Lesson of the Canton Uprising (Kuang-chou pao-tung chih i-i yü chiao-hsun 廣 州 暴 動 之 意 義 與 教 訓), 1927, 255.21/804/11790; and CCPCC, Resolutions on the Problems of Propaganda and Factionalism in the Party (Kuan-yü tang-nei hsuan-ch'uan p'ai-pieh wen-t'i chueh-i an 關 於 黨 內 宣 傳 派 別 問 題 決 議 案), 1929, 255.21/804/18403.

3. CCPCC, Second Plenum, Resolutions on Organizational Questions (Tsu-chih wen-t'i chueh-i an 組 織 問 題 決 議 案), July 9, 1929, 255.21/804/12058.

4. Summary of the Politburo Enlarged Meeting Held in March (Chuang-yang san-yueh cheng-chih-chü hui-i ti tsung-chieh 中 央 三 月 政 治 局 會 議 的 總 結), November 22, 1930, 255.21/809/2572.

5. Red Flag Daily (Hung-ch'i jih-pao 紅 旗 日 報), August-September 1930, no BIC number.

6. CCP Secretariat, Shanghai Tide (Hu-ch'ao 滬 潮), April-May 1930, 052.33/810/15632; Ho Tzu-shu (何 子 述), A Letter from Ho Tzu-shu to the Northern Bureau (Ho Tzu-shu chih pei-fang-chü ti hsin 何 子 述 致 北 方 局 的 信), 1930, 255.35/159/1119; also see Statement of the Views of Ho Meng-hsiung (Ho Meng-hsiung i-chien shu 何 孟 雄 意 見 書), Parts I-III, September-October 1930, BIC 262.9/159.

7. Central Correspondence (Chuang-yang t'ung-hsin [or t'ung-hsun] 中 央 通 信 [通 訊]), August 1927 to December 1927, in two volumes, 255.21/804 or 052.1/804.

8. Central Circular (Chung-yang t'ung-kao 中央通告),
1927-1932, perhaps two dozen in number, 262.3/804.

9. CCPCC, Organization Bureau, Organization Bulletin (Tsu-chih
t'ung-hsun 組織通訊), August 1929 et. seq.; also,
CCPCC, Organization Bureau, Organization Notification (Tsu-chih
t'ung-chih 組織通知), 1929, 255.24/811/9399.

10. Other documents essential for research on this period include
Transformations (Chuan-pien 轉變), Shanghai, 1933, BIC
245.3/815; Comintern Line (Kuo-chi lu-hsien 國際路線),
no date, BIC 300.3/809; and, CCPCC, Politburo, Resolution on
Comrade [Chang] Kuo-t'ao (Kuan-yü [Chang] Kuo-t'ao t'ung-chih
ti chueh-i 關於 [張] 國燾同志的決議),
December 16, 1930, BIC 262.07/809.

For a more comprehensive list of documents from this period
available at the BIC see, Richard C. Thornton, The Comintern
and the Chinese Communists, 1928-1931 (Seattle: University of
Washington Press, 1969), pp. 227-240.

11. CCPCC, Directives on Struggle Work (Tou-cheng kung-tso chih-
shih 鬥爭工作指示), 1932, 224.2/804/11736; CCPCC,
Outline of the Political Report (Cheng-chih pao-kao ta-kang
政治報告大綱), 1930, 257.1/804/9208; CCPCC, The Work
of [Party] Construction (Chien-she kung-tso 建設工作),
no date, 241/804/17922; CCPCC, Organization Bureau, Regulations
on Inspection Work by the Chinese Communist Central Committee
(Chung-kung chung-yang hsun-shih t'iao-chien 中共中央
巡視條件), 1932, 223/811/ 12103.

12. CCPCC, Chinese Communist Central Committee Documents
(Chung-kung chung-yang wen-chien 中共中央文件),
1932-1933, 052.1/809/2717 (or 297.4/811).

13. CCPCC, Letter to Comrades: Problems of Opposing and Eradi-
cating the Line of Comrade Li-san (Kao t'ung-chih shu: fan-tui
ho su-ch'ing Li-san t'ung-chih lu-hsien ti wen-t'i 告同志
書：反對和肅清立三同志路線的問題),
1931, 255.25/804/11420; CCPCC, *Resolutions Regarding the Development of Party Organization (Kuan-yü fa-chan tang ti tsu-chih
chueh-i an 關於發展黨的組織決議案),
1931, 255.21/804/10400-1.

14. Resolution of the Kiangsu Provincial Committee In Regard to the Expulsion of P'eng-Shu-chih, Wang Tse-k'ai, Ma Yü-fu, Ts'ai Chen-teh, and In Regard to the Opposition to Opportunism Within the Party and the Trotskyite Anti-Party Faction (Chiangsu sheng-wei wei k'ai-ch'u P'eng Shu-chih, Wang Tse-k'ai, Ma Yü-fu, Ts'ai Chen-teh, chi fan-tui tang-nei chi-hui-chu-i yü T'o-lo-ssu-chi fan-tui-p'ai chueh-i 江蘇省委為開除彭述之、汪澤愷、馬玉夫、蔡振德、及反對黨內機會主義與托洛斯基反對派決議), Kiangsu Provincial Committee, 1929, 263.3/806/12703.

15. CCPCC, Propaganda Bureau, Red Flag Weekly (Hung-ch'i chou-pao 紅旗周報), 1930-1933, 052.1/804.

16. CCPCC, Propaganda Bureau, Party Construction (Tang ti chien-she 黨的建設), January-April 1931, 12 issues, 052.1/804; the Bureau also holds two issues of a publication with the same title published by the Northern Fukien Committee. See Min-pei (閩北) Committee, Party Construction, May 1932, 052.1/804.

17. CCPCC, Propaganda Bureau, Struggle (Tou-cheng 鬥爭), 1932-1934, 052.1/809. Published in Shanghai until late 1933; not to be confused with periodical of the same title in the Central Soviet area.

18. T'ieh Ts'ui (鐵淬), "The Bolshevik Call and the Proletariat's Answer" ("Pu-er-sai-wei-k'e hao-chao yü wu-ch'an-chieh-chi ti hui-ta" 布爾塞維克號召與無產階級的回答), Struggle, November 18, 1932.

19. A sampling includes, Kiangsu Provincial Committee, Provincial Committee Circular, No. 15 (Sheng-wei t'ung-kao ti-shih-wu hao 省委通告第十五號), February 1930, 255.34/806/9312; Manchuria Provincial Committee, Letter to Oppressed Peasants of Manchuria (Kao ch'uan Man lao-k'u nung-min shu 告全滿勞苦農民書), 1930, 255.35/814/12415; Standing Committee of the Fukien Provincial Committee, Record of the Standing Committee (Ch'ang-wei hui-i chi-lu 常委會議紀錄), 1930, 255.4/811/11785; Western Kiangsi Action Committee,

Resolutions of an Enlarged Meeting of the Secretariat (Mi-shu-ch'u k'uo-ta hui-i chueh-i an 秘書處擴大會議決議案), 1930, 255.31/825/11271; Shensi Provincial Committee, Shensi Letter to the CCP Central Committee (Shan-hsi lai-hsin chih chung-kung chung-yang 陝西來信致中共中央), 1931, 255.35/810/117341; Northwest Anhwei Provincial Committee, Program for Correcting Work in Northwest Anhwei (Cheng-li Wan-hsi-pei kung-tso t'i-kang 整理皖西北工作提綱), 1932, 255.33/812/1112.

20. Kiangsu Provincial Committee, Lenin Life (Lieh-ning sheng-huo 列寧生活), 1932-1937, 052.1/806 et. seq.

21. Shensi Provincial Committee, Struggle and Study (Tou-cheng yü hsueh-hsi 鬥爭與學習), 1931, 052.1/808.

22. Fukien Red Flag (Fu-chien hung-ch'i 福建紅旗), 1931, no BIC number; also, see Southwest Fukien Provincial Committee, Red Flag, 1935, 12 issues, 052.1/813.

23. Unfortunately, it is difficult to identify the provincial origin of many of these documents because of their poor condition and/or lack of official labels.

24. Fukien Provincial Committee, Record of the Fifth Enlarged Executive Committee (Ti-wu tz'u shih-wei k'uo-ta-hui chi-lu 第五次執委擴大會紀錄), 1931, 255.32/813/11014.

25. Shensi Provincial Committee, Criticism and Self-Criticism (P'i-p'ing yü tzu-wo p'i-p'ing 批評與自我批評), no date, 244.2/810/17798-9.

26. A sampling of county materials includes, T'ung-shan County Committee, Resolutions on Work Plans of the First Enlarged Conference of Party Members (Ti-i tz'u tang-yuan tai-piao ta-hui kung-tso chi-hua chueh-i an 第一次黨員代表大會工作計劃決議案), 1932, 255.31/811/9298; Ta-yeh County Committee, Hupeh, Political Knowledge (Cheng-chih ch'ang-shih 政治常識), 1932, 244.3/803/9279; Hsia-chiang County Committee, Problems of Party Organization (Tang ti tsu-chih wen-t'i 黨的組織問題), 1930, 250/810/10402.

27. Amoy City Committee, <u>Outline of Mobilization</u> (Tung-yuan ta-kang 動員大綱), no date, 224/812/11008; Shao T'ai (紹泰), <u>Work Conditions in Tientsin</u> (T'ien-chin kung-tso ch'ing-hsing 天津工作情形), no date, 257.011/941/11943; Wuhu City Committee, <u>Letter from Wuhu to the Hsuan-ch'eng County Committee</u> (Wu-hu shih kei Hsuan-ch'eng hsien-wei hsin 蕪湖市給宣城縣委信), no date, 255.35/816/18427.

28. Shanghai Central District Committee, <u>Emergency Circular on How to Further Work in Connection with the Tragedy of Pao-shan Road</u> (Tsen-yang tso k'uo-ta Pao-shan-lu ts'an-an kung-tso chin-chi t'ung kao 怎樣作擴大寶山路慘案工作緊急通告), no date, 255.34/814/1958; Northern Fukien District Committee Party School, <u>Lecture Notes on Branch Work</u> (Chih-pu kung-tso chiang-i 支部工作講義), October 1932, 232.5/814.

29. See <u>Counties</u>, Glossary D.

30. Materials on file at the Bureau from counties in Anhwei, Kiang-su, and the O-Yü-Wan Soviet seem the most plentiful for this period.

31. <u>Draft Resolutions of the First Enlarged Meeting of the Liu-an County Committee</u> (Liu-an ch'uan-hsien wei-hui ti-i tz'u k'uo-ta hui chueh-i ts'ao-an 六安全縣委會第一次擴大會決議草案), 1931, 255.31/804/10386.

32. For the CCP see <u>Outline of a Discussion on the Problems in Opposing the Trotskyite Faction</u> (Fan-tui T'o-p'ai wen-t'i t'ao-lun ta-kang 反對托派問題討論大綱), no date, 262.39/804/1798; for the Trotskyites see <u>Alliance of Chinese Communism, The Death of the United-Front Stalinist Party</u> (Lien-ho chan-hsien Shih-t'ai-lin tang ti ssu-wang 聯合戰線史太林黨的死亡), 1937, 262.39/806/1760; for the Third Party see <u>Collection Concerning the Third Party</u> (Ti-san-tang shih-chi 第三黨事輯), 1933, 263.11/811/8444.

The most valuable materials on the Chinese Trotskyite movement are from the post-1937 period. For instance, there is

22

Cheng Hsueh-chia (鄭學稼), A Criticism of Mao Tse-tung
(P'i-p'ing Mao Tse-tung 批評毛澤束), 1943. However
according to Richard Kagan, this document may have been recently removed from the BIC.

33. Democratic Weekly (**Min-chu chou-k'an** 民主週刊),
Democratic Weekly Publishing Society, 1930, 052.9/805/10654.

34. O-Yü-Wan Soviet Government, Proclamation on Reforming the
Soviet Movement (Kai-tsao Su-wei-ai yun-tung hsuan-yen 改
造蘇維埃運動宣言), April 2, 1931, 224.1/812/
12487.

35. Hsiang-O-hsi Soviet Government, Correspondence of the Hsiang-
O-hsi and Min-hsi Soviet Districts (Hsiang-O-hsi yü Min-hsi
Su-ch'ü t'ung-hsin 湘鄂西與閩西蘇區通信),
no date, 255.35/812/9371.

36. O-hsi Soviet Government, Support the Special O-hsi District's
Third Representative Conference's Announcement to the Worker-
Peasant Masses (Yung-hu O-hsi t'e-pieh ch'ü, ti-san tz'u tai-
piao ta-hui kao kung-nung ch'ün-chung 擁護鄂西特
別區第三次代表大會告工農群眾),
1933, 255.35/812/11747.

37. Northeast Kiangsi Special Committee, The Duty and Task of
the Party in Reforming the Soviets (Tang tsai Su-wei-ai kai-
tsao chung ti jen-wu ho kung-tso 黨在蘇維埃改
造中的任務和工作), 1931, no BIC number.

38. Kan-hsi-nan Soviet Government, Soviet Provisional Political
Programs on Land (Su-wei-ai lin-shih t'u-ti cheng-kang 蘇
維埃臨時土地政網), July 1929, no BIC number.

39. Hsiao Tso-liang, The Land Revolution in China, 1930-1934
(Seattle: University of Washington Press, 1969).

40. Mien-yang County Political Bureau, Conclusions on the Problems
of the Soviets (Su-wei-ai wen-t'i chieh-lun 蘇維埃問
題結論), 1930, 255.31/807/11692.

41. Central Soviet Bureau, Political Resolutions (Cheng-chih chueh-

i an 政治決議案), 1932, 255.21/820/11701; Central
Soviet Bureau, Provisional Act to Reapportion the Administrative
Districts of the Chinese Soviet Republic (Chung-hua Su-wei-ai
kung-ho-kuo hua-fen hsing-cheng-ch'ü yü chan-hsing t'iao-li
中華蘇維埃共和國劃分行政區域
暫行條例), no date, 575.297/802.

42. CCPCC, Provisional Regulations on Organization for Various
Echelons of the Soviet Government (Ko-chi Su-wei-ai cheng-fu
chan-hsing tsu-chih t'iao-li 各級蘇維埃政府暫
行組織條例), November 1931, no BIC number.

43. CCPCC, *Communist (Kung-ch'an-tang jen 共產黨人),
Yenan, 1939, #1-4, and 12, 052.1/806.

44. Lo Fu (洛甫) [pseudonym for Chang Wen-t'ien], "The Rights
and Responsibilities of Communist Party Members" ("Kung-ch'an-
tang yuan ti ch'üan-li yü i-wü" 共產黨員的權利
與義務), Communist, September 1, 1939.

45. Ch'en Yun (陳雲), "Strengthen the Party's Work With the
Masses in the War Zones" ("Kung-ku tang yü chan-ch'ü ti ch'ün-
chung kung-tso" 鞏固黨與戰區的群眾工作),
Communist, September 1, 1939.

46. Yang Ying-chieh (楊英傑), "Class Relations and the People's
Livelihood in Three Villages of the Yu-chu District, Yen-ch'uan
County" ("Yen-ch'uan hsien Yu-chu ch'ü san-hsiang ti chieh-chi
kuan-hsi chi jen-min sheng-huo" 延川縣禹居區三鄉
的階級關係及人民生活), #3, Commu-
nist, December 1939.

47. Shen-Kan-Ning Committee, Unity (T'uan-chieh 團結), Yenan,
1938-1943, #5-6, 8-15, 24-26, 28 & 2:2-3, 9-11, 13, 052.1/805.

48. Chin-Ch'a-Chi Military District, New Great Wall (Hsin ch'ang-
ch'eng 新長城), Fu-p'ing, 1940, 052.1/813. This issue
includes a discussion of the CPSU Bolshevik Party history used
for cadre education in the Shen-Kan-Ning Border Region Assem-
bly; Chi-Lu-Yü Committee, Plains (P'ing-yuan 平原), #1,
1944, 052.1/805; the two editions of Plains published by the Chi-
Lu-Yü and South Hopeh Committees were completely separate.

The Bureau of Intelligence Library has three issues of the North China Bureau's Party Life (Tang ti sheng-huo 黨的生活). Number 6, for instance, has an important article on intraparty periodicals by Ch'en I.

49. Huai-pei, Su-Wan-Yü Committee, Dawn (Fo-hsiao 拂曉), 1943-1946, #1-5, 7, 9, 11-22, 24, 25, 27-32, 34, 052.1/820.

50. New Fourth Army, Chiang-pei Unit Party Committee, Party Life, (Tang-ti sheng-huo 黨的生活), 1941-1942, #1-5, 7, 9-10, 14, 17, 052.1/819.

51. Huai-pei Party Committee, *Party Bulletin (Tang-nei t'ung-hsun 黨內通訊), 1944-1946, #1-13, 16, 17, 052.1/811.

52. Pin-hai District Committee, Branch Bulletin (Chih-pu t'ung-hsun 支部通訊), 1947, #2, no BIC number; Chiang-huai Second District Committee (江淮第二區委), Huai-pei Bulletin (Huai-pei t'ung-hsun 淮北通訊), 1948, #1, no BIC number; Lu-Sui-T'ung District Committee, Mass Bulletin (Ch'ün-chung t'ung-hsun 群眾通訊), 1944, #1, no BIC number Lu-Sui-T'ung District Committee, War Life (Chan-tou sheng-huo 戰鬥生活), 1944, #8, no BIC number.

53. Central China Bureau, *Central China Bulletin (Hua-chung t'ung-hsun 華中通訊), 1946, #2-4, 6, 052.1/813; and New Fourth Army, Seventh Division, *Truth (Chen-li 真理), 1942-1944, #1, 11, 14, 16, no BIC number.

54. P'eng Teh-huai (彭德懷), "A Report on Work in the North China Base Area" ("Kuan-yü Hua-pei ken-chü-ti kung-tso ti pao-kao" 關於華北根據地工作的報告), Truth #14, August 1943.

55. Huai-nan, Su-Wan Party Committee, Huai-nan Party Magazine (Huai-nan tang-k'an 淮南黨刊), 1943-1945, #12-18; 052.1/820. A table of contents for the above periodicals may be found in Tokuda Noriyuki, "A List of Articles in Communist Periodicals in the Yenan Period" ("Yenan Jiki ni Okeru Chukyo Shuppan Zasshi Mokuroku" 延安時期に於る中共出版雜誌目錄, Asia Research (Asia Kenkyu アジア研究), XIII:3, October 1966, pp. 59-81.

56. Michael Lindsay, Notes on Educational Problems in Communist China (New York: Institute of Pacific Relations, 1950).

57. Boyd Compton, Mao's China: Party Reform Documents, 1942–1944 (Seattle: University of Washington Press, 1952).

58. Mark Selden, The Yenan Way in Revolutionary China, p. 177.

59. Mao Tse-tung, Economic Problems and Financial Problems (Ching-chi wen-t'i yü ts'ai-cheng wen-t'i 經濟問題與財政問題), Shanghai, Ho-chung Press, 1946, 213.11/43/7853; Jen Pi-shih, "An Opinion on Several Problems" ("Kuan-yü chi-ko wen-t'i ti i-chien" 關於幾個問題的意見), Dawn (拂曉), 1:1, 1-49; CCPCC, Northwest Bureau, Government Rectification Problems (Cheng-cheng wen-t'i 整政問題), May 1943, 255.23/187/8184; CCPCC, Northwest Bureau, Army Rectification Problems (Cheng-chün wen-t'i 整軍問題), May 1943, 209.807/447/3852; *CCPCC, Northwest Bureau, A General Summary on the Proceedings and Other Experiences of the Shen-Kan-Ning Border Region's Party Senior Cadre Conference (Kuan-yü Shan-Kan-Ning pien-ch'ü tang kao-kan-hui ching-kuo chi ch'i ching-yen ti tsung-chieh 關於陝甘寧邊區黨高幹會經過及其經驗的總結), June 1943, 256.1/806/3219; CCPCC, Northwest Bureau, On Correcting the Problems in Relationships Between the Various Organizations of the Party, Government, Army and Masses (Cheng-tun tang-cheng-chün-min ko tsu-chih chien kuan-hsi wen-t'i 整頓黨政軍民各組織間關係問題), May 1943, 256.1/278/3196; *CCPCC, Northwest Bureau, Comrade Kao Kang's Conclusions at the Northwest Bureau's Senior Cadre Conference (Kao Kang t'ung-chih tsai hsi-pei-chü kao-kan-hui shang ti chieh-lun 高崗同志在西北局高幹會上的結論), October 20, 1943, 255.3/278/2136; *CCPCC, Northwest Bureau, An Examination of the Historical Problems of the Party in the Border Regions (Pien-ch'ü tang ti li-shih wen-t'i 邊區黨的歷史問題), June 1943, 255.33/806/5994.

60. Central Kiangsu Committee, *Reference Materials on the Three Rectifications (Cheng-tun san feng ti ts'an-k'ao ts'ai-liao 整頓三風的參考材料), 1943, #1, 6 & 10, 256.1/577.

The Three Rectifications were in study (hsueh-feng), the Party (tang-feng), and writing style (wen-feng). The first rectification consisted of an attack on "subjectivism," that is, the failure to thoroughly investigate and research concrete conditions, thereby causing a failure to carry out policy; the second on "sectarianism," which was the cadres' inability to put into practice party programs and their tendency to fear mass criticism; and, the third concerned stereotyped writings (namely, the eight-legged essay) and, more generally, "red-tapism" (wen-pan) in government activities.

61. Chi-Lu-Yü Administrative Office, *Rectification Guide (Cheng-feng chih-tao 整風指導), 1943, #1 & 2, 256.1/726/3203.

62. CCPCC, Politburo, *Rectification Collection (Cheng-feng hui-k'an 整風彙刊), no date, 256.1/809; essays by Chang Wen-t'ien (張聞天) include "On the Nature and Use of Investigation Work," "On the Party's Two Styles of Work Methods," and "Sympathize More with the Basic Problems of the Masses."

63. Chi-Lu-Yü, Sixth District Party Committee, Propaganda Bureau, How to Carry Out Rectification Study (Ju-ho chin-hsing cheng-feng hsueh-hsi 如何進行整風學習), 1943, 256.1/816.

64. Tseng Mien (曾勉), Rectification Reference Materials (Cheng-feng ts'an-k'ao ts'ai-liao 整風參政材料), 1944, 256.1/337/3177.

65. Chang Chih-chi (張之吉), Rectification Notes (Cheng-feng pi-chi 整風筆記), no date, handwritten, 256.1/369/3192; and Chang K'ai (張凱), Rectification Notes (Cheng-feng pi-chi 整風筆記), no date, handwritten, 256.1/369/8214.

66. *Rectification Documents (Cheng-feng wen-chien 整風文件), Chi-Lu-Yü Bookstore, 1944, 256.1/372/3173.

67. Behind the Scenes of the Recent Communist Internal Party Struggle (Chung-kung tsui-chin tang-nei tou-cheng nei-mu 中共最近黨內鬥爭內幕), Unity Press, ed., 1944, 256.1; *A View of the Many Facets of the Communists' Three

Rectifications Movement (Chung-kung san-feng yun-tung chih mien mien-kuan 中共三風運動之面面觀), Unity Press, ed., 1942, 256.1/577.

68. A Direction for Literary and Art Workers (Wen-i kung-tso-che ti fang-hsiang 文藝工作者的方向), Dawn Press, ed., 1942, 649/43/2257.

69. Wang Shih-wei (王實味), The Wild Lily (Yeh pai-ho hua 野百合花), Chungking, 256.1/23/237. A Nationalist reprint of original articles from Liberation Daily.

70. *Chou Yang (周揚), Manifestation of a New Era for the Masses (Piao-hsien hsin ti ch'ün-chung ti shih-tai 表現 新的群眾的時代), 1945, 649/203/3684; *On the Ideology of Wang Shih-wei (Lun Wang Shih-wei ti ssu-hsiang i-chih 論王實味的思想意識), Chi-Lu-Yü Bookstore, 1944, no BIC number.

71. *"The Wild Lily" and Others: The True Impression of Yenan's New Literature ("Yeh pai-ho hua" chi ch'i-ta: Yen-an hsin wen-hsueh chen-hsiang 《野百合花》及其他：延安新 文學真象), Unity Press, ed., 1943, 256.1/812/7419; and see Liberation Daily, June 15, 16, 17, & 20, and July 3 & 4, 1942.

72. CCPCC, Southern Bureau, Communist Party Member Textbooks (Kung-ch'an-tang-yuan k'o-pen 共產黨員課本), 1952, 244.3/804/19406.

73. Liao-yang City Party Committee, Political Study Reference Materials (Cheng-chih hsueh-hsi ts'an-k'ao ts'ai-liao 政 治學習參考材料), 1948, 244.3/816/6615.

74. How to Carry Out Theoretical Study (Tsen-yang chin-hsing li-lun hsueh-hsi), Shanghai, 1954, 244/810/21804.

75. Lectures on Basic Knowledge for Chinese Communist Party Members (Chung-kuo kung-ch'an-tang tang-yuan chi-pen chih-shih chiang-hua 中國共產黨黨員基本知識 講話), Wuhan Marxism-Leninism School, 1952, 244.3/868/ 19510.

28

76. How to Study Documents (Tsen-yang hsueh-hsi wen-chien 怎
     樣學習文件), 1950, 244/522/0033; Study and Practice
     (Hsueh-hsi yü shih-chien 學習與實踐), 1941, 244/536/
     2275; Research on Work Methods (Kung-tso fang-fa yen-chiu
     工作方法研究), 1953, 244/340/19843.

77. Ts'ao Po-han (曹伯韓), Textbook on Propaganda Methods
     (Hsuan-ch'uan chi-shu tu-pen 宣傳技術讀本), Hankow,
     1938, 253/348/2344; CCPCC, Northwest Bureau, Propaganda
     Department, A Notification on Strenthening Communication Work
     in Various Counties (Kuan-yü chia-ch'iang ko-hsien t'ung-hsun
     kung-tso ti t'ung-chih 關於加強各縣通訊工
     作的通知), no date, 253/806/6183; T'ai County Committee,
     Propaganda Bureau, What We Ought to Propagandize Now (Mu-
     ch'ien hsu-yao hsuan-ch'uan shen-ma 目前需要宣傳
     什麼), no date, 253/810/6203.

78. Propaganda Handbook (Hsuan-ch'uan shou-ts'e 宣傳手冊),
     Shanghai, 1951, 253.12/809/21582; How to Be a Propaganda
     Worker (Tsen-ma-yang tso hsuan-ch'uan yuan 怎麼樣作
     宣傳員), Peking, 1951, 253.1/832/0541.

79. Feng Pai-chü (馮白駒), The Glory of the Chinese Com-
     munist Party is Shining on Hainan Island (Chung-kuo kung-ch'an-
     tang ti kuang-yao chao-yao tsai Hai-nan tao shang 中國共
     產黨的光耀照耀在海南島上), Canton:
     South China People's Publishing Society, 1951, 232.1137/387/
     23694.

80. Ministry of Defense, How to Establish a Taiwan People's Guer-
     rilla Force (Tsen-yang chien-li T'ai-wan jen-men ti yu-chi wu-
     chuang 怎樣建立臺灣人民的游擊武裝),
     1950, 276/739/828; Bureau of Investigation, Records from the
     Communist Bandit's Taiwan Provincial Committee (Fei T'ai-
     kung sheng-wei shu-chi 匪台共省委書記), 1954,
     232.1132/725/221304; also see The League of the Taiwanese
     Masses (臺灣民眾聯盟), A Way Out for Taiwan
     (T'ai-wan ti ch'u-lu 臺灣的出路), Hong Kong, no date
     263.3307/805/7416, 22095.

81. Shanghai Evening News (Shang-hai wan-pao 上海晚報);
     Yin-ch'uan Daily (Yin-ch'uan jih-pao 銀川日報); Ch'engtu
     Daily (Ch'eng-tu jih-pao 成都日報); Pao-t'ou Daily (Pao-

t'ou jih-pao 包頭日報); Sian Daily (Hsi-an jih-pao 西安日報); Nanking Daily (Nan-ching jih-pao 南京日報); Harbin Daily (Ha-erh-pin jih-pao 哈爾濱日報); Yunnan Daily (Yun-nan jih-pao 雲南日報); Sinkiang Daily (Hsin-chiang jih-pao 新疆日報): and Inner Mongolian Daily (Nei-meng-ku jih-pao 內蒙古日報). According to the Bureau's staff, holdings of these various newspapers are usually limited to short periods. The staff can suggest newspapers of possible interest, and displays in the Bureau's exhibition rooms can give an idea of the newspapers available.

82. Highest-level Directives (Tsui-kao chih-shih 最高指示), no date, no BIC number.

83. Reference News [Restricted] (Ts'an-k'ao hsiao-hsi 參考消息), 1971, no BIC number.

84. Documents of the Chinese Communist Party Central Committee (Chung-kung chung-yang wen-chien 中共中央文件), 1972, no BIC number.

85. Political Work Bulletin (Cheng-kung t'ung-hsun 政工通訊), 1972, no BIC number.

A SUPPLEMENTARY LIST OF SOURCES ON THE
CHINESE COMMUNIST PARTY AVAILABLE AT THE BIC*

CCPCC, Resolutions on Work Concerning the Reactionary Faction
in Chekiang (Fan-tung-p'ai Che-chiang kung-tso chueh-i an 反動
派 浙 江 工 作 決 議 案), 1927, 282/804/9210.

Manchuria Provincial Committee, A Report and Discussion of the
Manchurian Question (Man-chou wen-t'i pao-kao chi t'ao-lun 滿 洲
問 題 報 告 及 討 論), 1930, 255.33/814/11579; and Wuhan
City Committee, Wuhan City Committee Notification (Wu-han shih t'ung-
chih 武 漢 市 通 知), 1931, 255.34/808/9166.

Mien-yang County Soviet Government, Economic Committee 沔陽
縣 蘇 維 埃 政 府 經 濟 委 員 會), Handbook of Economic Tables
(Ching-chi tui-chao ts'e 經 濟 對 照 冊), 1930, 258.3/807/9311.

Hupeh-Anhwei Provisional Provincial Committee, Resolution on
the Work of the Hupeh-Anhwei Border Area's Provisional Provincial
Committee (O-Wan pien lin-shih sheng-wei kung-tso chueh-i an 鄂
皖 邊 臨 時 省 委 工 作 決 議 案), 1932, 255.31/812/
17823.

Fukien Provincial Committee, Resolutions of the Fourth Plenum
and the Problems of Intra-Party Struggle (Ssu chung ch'uan-hui yü tang-
nei tou-cheng wen-t'i chueh-i an 四 中 全 會 與 黨 內 鬥
爭 問 題 決 議 案), 1933, 257.532/815/12723.

Chahar Provincial Committee, Report on Work at the Front
(Ch'ien-hsien kung-tso pao-kao 前 綫 工 作 報 告), 1933,
257.532/815/12723.

Chang Wei-chih (張 維 之), Joint Letter to the Various
County Heads (Chih ko hsien hsien-chang lien-hsi hsin 致 各
縣 縣 長 聯 系 信), no date, 255.35/369/12033.

Hupeh Provincial Committee, Letter from the Hupeh Provincial
Committee to the West Hupeh Special Committee (Hu-pei sheng-wei
kei O-hsi t'e-wei hsin 湖 北 省 委 給 鄂 西 特 委 信),
no date, 255.35/812/9164.

* These are additional documents on the CCP to which there is no
reference in the text.

31

Political Department of the Third Pohai District, Lecture Materials for Branch Committee Cell Leaders (Chih-wei hsiao-tsu chang chiang-hua ts'ai-liao 支委 小組長 講話材料), no date, 232.5/812/2630.

CCPCC, Decisions on Techniques of Secret Documents and Secret Work in Regard to Organizational Problems (Mi-mi wen-chien, mi-mi kung-tso chi-shu kuan-yü tsu-chih wen-t'i ti chueh-ting 祕密文件，祕密工作技術關於組織問題的決定), no date, 276/804/8240.

Central Investigation and Statistical Bureau, Second Collection of Chinese Communist Secret Documents (Chung-kung mi-mi wen-chien chih erh 中共 祕密文件之二), no date, 276/815/7135.

Central Investigation and Statistical Bureau, Two Years of the CCP, From 1931 to 1933 (Tzu 1931 nien chih 1933 nien liang-nien lai chih Chung-kuo kung-ch'an-tang 自 1931 年至 1933 年 兩年來之中國共產黨), no date, no BIC number.

Hsiang-O-Kan Soviet Committee, Questions and Answers on Opposing Rich Peasants (Fan-tui fu-nung wen-ta 反對富農 問答), 1931, 244.3/812/11110.

O-Yü-Wan Soviet, Cultural Committee, Political Education Text (Cheng-chih chiao-pen 政治教本), 1931, 244.3/812/9256.

North Fukien Soviet, Labor Protection Bureau, Questions and Answers on Liquidating Counterrevolutionaries (Su fan wen-ta 肅反問答), 1932, 244.3/814/11181.

CCPCC, Hsiang-Kan Special Committee, Outline of Branch Work (Chih-pu kung-tso ta-kang 支部工作大綱), 1939 ?, 232.5/ 812/2623.

CCPCC, Propaganda Bureau, Branch Work, (Chih-pu kung-tso 支部工作), 1939, 232.5/804/2622.

CCPCC, Secretariat, Directive on Education for In-Service Cadres (Kuan-yü tsai-chih kan-pu chiao-yü ti chih-shih 關於在職 幹部教育的指示), March 20, 1940, 244.2/804/10826.

CCPCC, Chi-Chin Committee, Propaganda Bureau, Basic Educational Materials for Branches (Chih-pu chi-pen chiao-ts'ai 支部基本教材), September 1940, 244.3/816/1951.

CCPCC, Chi-Chin Committee, Propaganda Bureau, Educational Materials for Branch Party Members (Chih-pu tang-yuan chiao-ts'ai 支部黨員教材), 1945, 244.3/816/1939.

CCPCC, Chi-chung Ninth Sub-District Committee, Basic Information for Party Members (Tang-yuan chi-pen chih-shih 黨員 基本知識), 1945, 244.3/816/2587.

CCPCC, A Report Concerning the Party's Work Among the Masses--A New Strategy (Kuan-yü tang yü ch'ün-chung kung-tso ti pao-kao--hsin ts'e-lueh 關於黨與群眾工作的報告-- 新策略), 1937, 256.2/812/8719.

CCPCC, Organization Bureau, Directive on Principles of Local Work in the War of Resistance (Kuan-yü k'ang-chan chung ti fang kung-tso ti yuan-tse chih-shih 關於抗戰中地方工作的 原則知識), August 12, 1937, no BIC number.

CCPCC, Central China Bureau, How to Unite--The Strategy of Friendly Army Work (Ju-tz'u t'uan-chieh--yu-chün kung-tso chih ts'e-lueh 如此團結--友軍工作之策略), July 1940, 590.82/842/9706.

CCPCC, Propaganda Bureau, Discussion Outline of the Conference of Representatives of North China's Various Provincial Committees (Kuan-yü pei-fang ko sheng-wei tai-piao lien-hsi hui-i ti t'ao-lun ta-kang 關於北方各省委代表聯席會議的討論 大綱), no date, no BIC number.

CCPCC, Women's Movement Committee, Directive on the Direction and Responsibilities of the Present Women's Movement (Kuan-yü mu-ch'ien fu-nü yun-tung ti fang-chen ho jen-wu ti chih-shih hsin 關於目前婦女運動的方針和任務的指 示信), 1939, 544.5822/812/3629.

CCPCC, Chin-Ch'a-Chi Committee, On the Experience of Rectifying Party Branches (Kuan-yü cheng-li chih-pu ti ching-yen 關於 整理支部的經驗), 1941 ?, 232.5/810/2524.

34

New Fourth Army, Seventh Division, Political Department, <u>Cadre</u> <u>Cultural Text</u> (Kan-pu wen-hua k'o-pen 幹部文化課本), no date, 244.3/732/3748.

South Hopeh Military District, Political Department, <u>Party Mem-</u> <u>ber Text</u> (Tang-yuan k'o-pen 黨員課本), no date, 244.3/746/ 1931.

18th District Committee, (Chin-Chi-Lu-Yü?) Propaganda Bureau, <u>One-Thousand Character Text for Party Members</u> (Tang-yuan ch'ien- <u>tzu k'o-pen</u> 黨員千字課本), no date, 244.3/802/2589.

East Hopeh Committee, Propaganda Bureau, <u>Literacy Text for</u> <u>Party Members</u> (Tang-yuan shih-tzu k'o-pen 黨員識字課本), no date, 244.3/804/1913.

CCPCC, Politburo, <u>Resolutions on the Expulsion of Chang? ?</u> (Kuan-yü k'ai-ch'u Chang? ? ti chueh-i 關於開除張?? 的決議), 1931, 245.2/809/12480.

Yenan General Headquarters, Commander-In-Chief General Chu <u>Teh, Proclamation of Instructions</u> (Yen-an tsung-pu, Chu Teh tsung ssu-ling, fa-pu ming-ling 延安總部朱德總司令發佈 命令), August 2, 1945, no BIC number.

II. MASS MOVEMENTS

An attractive aspect of the BIC is its documentation of the CCP's programs of social and political action generally and, more particularly, of mass mobilization. Documents such as policy statements from the Central Committee and other Party units, work outlines distributed to cadres, reports from the field, as well as biographies and memoirs combine to give a full picture of the conception and implementation of Communist programs designed to win the support of the Chinese people. In addition, the documentation provides new perspectives on the evolution of the mass line as the CCP's primary technique for building a mass base during the War of Resistance.

A. The Labor Movement

The commitment of the CCP leaders to Marxist-Leninist ideology is reflected in their consistent effort to mobilize China's relatively small working class. Before Mao's rise to the Party's leadership in 1935, the Central Committee and the CCP-affiliated All China General Labor Union formulated policies which treated the proletariat as the Party's main constituency in the revolutionary movement.[1] Of special interest in the BIC are several reports on the organization of labor unions--particularly in Shanghai[2]--which could be used to evaluate the leadership's understanding of Marxist-Leninist theory in developing a labor policy. Other documents could help scholars determine the extent of the Communist International's influence on the ideology of the CCP during the period. For instance, there are the Profintern-sponsored Bulletin of the Pacific Workers (T'ai-p'ing-yang kung-pao),[3] and the Far Eastern Worker (Yuan-tung kung-jen).[4] The latter was a publication of the Secretariat of the Pan-Pacific Labor Conference (T'ai-p'ing-yang lao-tung ta-hui mi-shu-ch'u), first established in Hankow in May 1927.

On a more practical level, accounts of the day-to-day problems confronting local Party units in rebuilding the labor movement from 1927 to 1930 can be found in Worker Bulletin (Kung-jen t'ung-hsun).[5] Even more important in this regard are several handwritten reports on the labor movement in Shanghai[6] and union organization among China's maritime workers.[7] These include open discussions of the CCP's policies and organization vis-à-vis the urban proletariat and frank evaluations of cadre work style and the effectiveness of Communist propaganda. In addition, many of the periodicals described in the section on Party Affairs, such as Red Flag Weekly, Lenin Life, and Struggle, treat the labor movement during the last few years of the CCP's urban operations, from 1930 to 1933. [8] Lenin Life, for instance, offers numerous articles and policy statements on the Kiangsu Provincial Committee's efforts at promoting strikes among Shanghai workers during the height of the Kuomintang's "white terror." [9]

Following the CCP's shift to the rural bases and Soviets in the early 1930s, the Communist labor movement lost much of its proletarian flavor. Unions enrolled not only production workers, but also handicraft workers, hired hands in agriculture, shop clerks, and craft apprentices. The war with Japan in 1937 and the expansion of rural resistance bases further accelerated this change. In 1939, for instance, statistics showed that in the Chin-Ch'a-Chi Border Region labor union, only twelve percent of the membership were classified as production workers. This twelve percent, moreover, was not the urban proletariat which Marx envisioned as leading the socialist revolution; instead it comprised peasants who worked in the mines or government factories during the winter and tended their fields the rest of the year. [10] Regarding the labor movement during the War of Resistance, the BIC has scattered reports and conference records from the North China bases and Shen-Kan-Ning, [11] and a particularly interesting discussion of the labor movement in the Chin-Chi-Yü Border Region. [12] An important source is the periodical, China Worker (Chung-kuo kung-jen) published in Yenan. [13] It includes a variety of articles from all of the North China base areas and some interesting local case studies of the working class.

One such study concerns the Ling-shan mines in Ch'ü-yang, Hopeh. These coal mines were originally part of a Sung dynasty porcelain complex in West Hopeh, which flourished until the region was depopulated during rebellion at the time of the establishment of the Ming dynasty. By 1939, only four mines were still operating, and they were all small operations financed through local capital. One mine had about 400 share holders, including some miners and the deity of a local temple, but only 5,000 yuan in capital. Tung Hsin, the survey's author, observed that only ten percent of the miners relied solely on the mines for a living, and of the remainder some owned as much as 20 mou of land and were independent farmers. Tung described the labor conditions, the system of contract and payment, and child labor and health problems, and also included statistics on local price fluctuations of food crops and goods over the past decade (1930-1939). The central discussion of the study concerned the development of the labor union movement after June 1937 and discussed union membership, programs and organizational activities. The depth of the article and the author's knowledge of local conditions bear out the importance which Party leaders attached to local information for the formulation of a labor policy.

In late 1945, the Communists captured Kalgan in southern Chahar Province and reactivated urban labor activities there.[14] By 1949-1950, the CCP was rebuilding the labor movement in much of North and Central China. The BIC has a number of interesting material produced by the old centers of labor radicalism, such as union handbooks,[15] critiques of cadre work style,[16] and discussions of the economic and cultural state of the workers.[17]

B. The Peasant Movement

By 1933, the Nationalists had driven the CCP from the cities, but then the Communists turned to develop a power base among the peasantry. This was not an entirely new direction, as advocates of peasant radicalism, such as P'eng P'ai and Mao Tse-tung, had maintained that the peasants were a potent revolutionary force in the 1920s. The BIC has only a scattering of documents on the land reforms and the peasant movement of the Kiangsi period (1931-1934).[18] The most important sources come from the War of Resistance and the Civil War, such as documents on the wartime peasant associations, the rent and reduction drives--especially from 1942 to 1945--and the land reform programs of the Civil War.

Materials on the peasant associations come from a number of base areas and include work outlines,[19] cadre lectures,[20] reports from the field,[21] reference materials,[22] and peasant association manuals.[23] Some, particularly association member handbooks and the "social education" texts for adult studies,[24] may be useful sources in separating the social impact of the Communist programs from their appeal to national mobilization against Japan. According to P'eng Teh-huai, during the War of Resistance the Communists retained their commitment to eradicate powerful "feudal" influences like superstition and filial piety by raising the peasants' political awareness.[25] As one peasant association handbook put it, "The Communist Party and the peasant association are not open to every poor, oppressed farmer, but only to those who understand that fate and bad luck are not the causes of social inequities."[26] The peasant associations' educational materials, used in conjunction with existing studies of peasant life before the revolution, are good sources for evaluating this new, popularized political ideology in terms of the traditional beliefs of Chinese peasants.[27]

Regarding agrarian policy, the Communists, in 1937, modified previous programs calling for a radical redistribution of land and adopted more moderate proposals for rent and interest reductions. The BIC lacks materials from the earlier work in rent and interest reduction, but has a number of interesting documents published following the Politburo's directive on land policy in the base areas of January 1942.[28] These sources include an important report on the Party's agrarian movement from the T'ai-hang District (southeast Shansi),[29] an unusual discussion from the Tung-chiang (Kwangtung) base area[30]--unusual, because of the rarity of extant materials from this region--and several collections of laws and regulations on rent and interest reduction.[31]

In April 1945, as victory over Japan seemed assured, the CCP returned to the more radical policy of "land to the tillers." The new program was uniform throughout China but was applied in accordance with the length of time a particular region had been under Communist control. In areas that had recently come under Communist rule, the Party introduced only the moderate rent reduction programs; but in the old base areas such as Chin-Ch'a-Chi the Party forced the gentry to sell a good portion of their land to the landless tenants and called for income redistribution through a "settling of accounts" (ch'ing-suan). The diversity in local situations led to a classification of different areas and the creation of models to serve as case studies and guides for cadres in other districts. According to Mao Tse-tung's preface to a discussion of the experiences of Kuo County (hsien), Shansi there were three basic models for land reform in this period.[32]

Materials in the BIC on land reform after 1945 include a 200-page report from the T'ai-hang District on organizing the land reform movement and a 42-page account from a South Hopeh District on variations in the practice of land reform between recently liberated regions (after 1945) and the old, wartime base areas.[33] The Central Shantung

Committee issued an instruction to cadres on how to lead the masses
"to turn the tables on the upper classes and achieve a new life" (fan-
shen) through land reform;[34] and there is a lengthy description on
"settling of accounts" with landlords in Chi-Lu-Yü.[35] One rather
unusual document is a Land Reform Guide from Hainan Island.[36] In
addition, there are several documents on land redistribution programs
from the 1947-1948 period,[37] and a few on land reform in the first
days of the People's Republic.[38] Material in the BIC on agrarian
policy is sufficient to support a detailed study of Communist work
in this area from 1942 to 1949, and includes many documents that
are not available elsewhere.

A number of documents on the CCP's policies toward the peasantry discuss mass work and the principles of mass line leadership.
The debate among scholars over the nature of the Communist appeal
during the War of Resistance has been going on for over ten years;[39]
but not until recently have scholars pointed to the mass line as a major
factor in Communist successes during the war with Japan.[40] The Bureau's materials detail the origins and development of the mass line
from both an organizational and theoretical perspective. Local party
directives,[41] cadre study materials,[42] lecture outlines from Resistance
University (K'ang-ta),[43] and regional reports[44] are some of the more
valuable documents which touch on this subject. Used in conjunction
with internal Party study materials, publications of mass organizations,
and military manuals on mass mobilization,[45] they reveal the Communist approach to the organization and political mobilization of the Chinese peasantry at the most practical level of work. These documents
demonstrate the consistent, long-term development and application of
techniques which the CCP canonized in the phrase "From the masses,
to the masses" in the June 1943 Central Committee directive, "Some
Questions Concerning Methods of Leadership."[46]

C. Women and Youth

In addition to the economic classes of the workers and peasants,
the CCP sought to draw on the revolutionary aspirations of other groups.
The vigor of youth and the particularly oppressed position of women in
Chinese society prompted special attention by the Party. On their role
in the revolutionary struggle, there are from the 1930s and 1940s numerous Central Committee directives, provincial committee communi-
ques, and special conference decisions which outline CCP policy.[47]

Most valuable are the specialized journals dealing with various social, economic, and political aspects of these two movements. For instance, in the early 1930s, Women's Life (Fu-nü sheng-huo) published articles dealing with the special problems of organizing women workers, and served as a forum for criticizing tendencies toward discrimination by their male counterparts in the CCP.[48] In the same period, the CCP's Youth League published journals at the central and provincial levels, with titles such as Lenin Youth (Lieh-ning ch'ing-nien)[49] and Vanguard (Hsien-feng),[50] dealing with the recruitment and training of potential Party members. The latter includes a series of articles critical of Communist Youth League (CYL) branch work and of the members' inability to plan their operations in line with "mass psychology."[51]

From the War of Resistance there is a particularly rich collection of periodicals available at the BIC. China Women (Chung-kuo fu-nü) was the major publication of the period and includes articles by leading figures in the women's movement such as K'ang K'o-ch'ing, Ch'en Ch'ang-hao, and Liu Ying.[52] For instance, problems in mobilizing China's "broken shoes" (p'o-hsieh), that is, prostitutes, for patriotic action is confronted in one series of articles and offers a unique perspective on the CCP's appeal to eléments déclassés in Chinese society.[53] In China Youth (Chung-kuo ch'ing-nien) there are equally important articles published by veterans of the December Ninth Movement (1935-1936), such as Huang Hua and Li Ch'ang;[54] and there is considerable material on the training of Party cadres for work among youth.[55]

Most of the BIC's documentation on the youth movement comes from the Communist Youth League. But for the years 1936 to 1945 there is considerable material issued by various youth national salvation groups, which were organized separately in areas of Communist activity following the abolition of the CYL in 1936. The earliest of these was the National Liberation Vanguards of China (Chung-kuo min-tsu chieh-fang hsien-feng-tui).[56] It was formed in February 1936 in response to the anti-Japanese demonstrations by student activists in Peiping, Tientsin, and other major Chinese cities during the previous December. The Vanguards remained the leading CCP youth group until late 1939, when various youth associations became the Communists' principal organizations for wartime mobilization of youth.[57] There are over twenty documents in the BIC on the Vanguards. Some are only broadsheets, work outlines, or propaganda manifestos, but there are also several tracts of considerable length.[58]

After 1949, as the CCP built up its organizational base throughout the country, Chinese youth and women became an even more important base for recruiting Party members. How to Be a Youth League Member, for example, describes the educational and political training of youth in Hankow designed to prepare them for full Party membership.[59] And, for a look into the special problems of women workers in the new China of the 1950s, the Handbook on Work Among Women Workers includes a number of volumes.[60]

D. The Sacrifice League

Although not officially tied to the Chinese Communist Party, the Shansi Sacrifice League (Shan-hsi hsi-sheng t'ung-meng-hui) was an important organization for the mobilization of Shansi youth and peasants in united front activities during the early days of the war with Japan.[61] Yen Hsi-shan, the Shansi warlord, organized the group in September 1936, in coordination with local Communist leaders such as Po I-po, Sung Shao-wen, and others, to mobilize anti-Japanese sentiments and oppose Japanese advances against the province of Suiyuan, then under Shansi's domination through Yen's subordinate, Fu Tso-i. After war began in July 1937, the League became an important resistance force in Shansi through its military arm, the Dare-to-Die Corps (Chueh-ssu-tui).

The Sacrifice League leaders were young and generally inclined toward the Communist wartime programs; thus the League gradually gravitated towards the Communist cause. Alarmed by the growing Communist sympathies, Yen Hsi-shan attempted to gain control of the Dare-to-Die Corps, but this led to a rupture between Yen and the League in the Shansi New Army Incident in November 1939. The Sacrifice League and its army comprised an independent force after the incident, but its senior cadres were Communists, and they served as leading figures in the Communist sponsored Chin-Sui and Chin-Chi-Yü Border Regions.

The BIC holds a number of documents from the Sacrifice League not available in the West. Most of these originate from Hsia County, Shansi, a major Sacrifice League center. There are political handbooks,[62] manuals on mass work,[63] propaganda tracts,[64] and branch work outlines.[65] One of the more important sources is a brief history of the League by Po I-po.[66] The Bureau also has several tracts on

Sacrifice League activities published by the Yellow River Press, including a detailed account by Shih Pin on early League work in the Shansi mass movement.[67] In addition there are several issues of the Dare-to-Die Corps, 10th Column, Political Department magazine, Sentinel (Ch'ien-shao).[68]

FOOTNOTES TO CHAPTER II

1. Jean Chesneaux, The Chinese Labor Movement (Stanford: Stanford University Press, 1958).

2. For example, see CCPCC, Present and Future General Work Policy of the Shanghai Workers' Movement (Shang-hai chih-kung yun-tung chin-hou kung-tso tsung fang-chen 上海職工運動今後工作總方針), 1927, 556.282/804; and All China General Labor Union, Resolutions of the Fifth Labor Congress (Ti-wu tz'u lao-tung ta-hui chueh-i an 第五次勞動大會決議案), 1930, 556.1813/804/5597.

3. Pacific Red Mutual Aid Society (Profintern), Bulletin of the Pacific Workers (T'ai-p'ing-yang kung-pao 太平洋公報), 1929, 052.9/804/7657.

4. Secretariat of the Pan-Pacific Labor Conference, Far Eastern Worker (Yuan-tung kung-jen 遠東工人), 1929, no BIC number.

5. Worker Bulletin (Kung-jen t'ung-hsun 工人通訊), Shanghai, 1930, 052.33/803/9173 et. seq.

6. Report on Kiangsu by the All China General Labor Union (Ch'uan-kuo tsung-kung hui kuan-yü Chiang-su chih pao-kao 全國總工會關於江蘇之報告), 1929, 556.1812/806/3588.

7. All China General Labor Union, General Report of Last Year's Work Among Maritime Workers in Shanghai and Other Areas (Shang-hai teng ti hai-yuan kung-tso kuo-ch'ü i-nien lai tsung pao-kao 上海等地海員工作過去一年來總報告), 1929, 556.14/812/1493.

8. See Party Affairs, ff. 15, 16, & 17.

9. See, for instance, "Apply the Youth Corps' Best Experiences to Union Work" ("Chiang t'uan kung-tso chung tsui-hao ti ching-yen ying-yung tao kung-hui kung-tso chung-ch'ü" 將團工作中最好的經驗應用到工會工作中去), Lenin Life, December 5, 1932.

44

10. See "Workers of the Chin-Ch'a-Chi Border Region in the Midst of Struggle" ("Tsai tou-cheng chung ti Chin-Ch'a-Chi pien-ch'ü kung-jen" 在鬥爭中的晉察冀邊區工人), Liberation (Chieh-fang), #94, January 30, 1940.

11. Southeast Shansi General Labor Union, Conference on the Formation of a General Labor Union (Tsung-hui ch'eng-li ta-hui 總會成立大會), 1939, 556.13/810/3615; CCPCC, Speeches and Addresses of the Shen-Kan-Ning Border Region First Representative Conference (Shan-Kan-Ning pien-ch'ü ti-i tz'u tai-piao ta-hui hsuan-yen 陝甘寧邊區第一次代表大會宣言), 1938, 556/808/3573; Central Hopeh General Labor Union, Several Tasks the Central Hopeh Union Ought to Carry Out (Chi-chung kung-hui hsu-yao chih-hsing ti chi-ko kung-tso 冀中工會需要執行的幾個工作), no date, 556.18/816/2673.

12. Yang Yu (楊珏), The Workers Movement in the Chin-Chi-Yü Border Region (Chin-Chi-Yü pien-ch'ü ti kung-jen yun-tung 晉冀豫邊區的工人運動), 1941, T'ai-hang Masses Series #1, 556.282/470/3591.

13. China Worker (Chung-kuo kung-jen 中國工人), Yenan, New China Bookstore, 1940-1941, #1-9, 11-13, 052.33/804.

14. Documents in the BIC seized during the fall of Kalgan to the Nationalists in 1947 come from the education and industrial departments of the Chin-Ch'a-Chi Border Government, the Communist provisional government of Chahar, and include texts used in primary and middle schools, and newspapers, such as the Chin-Ch'a-Chi Daily (Chin-Ch'a-Chi jih-pao 晉察冀日報), 1946, no BIC number.

15. Shanghai General Labor Union, Handbook on Union Work (Kung-hui kung-tso shou-ts'e 工會工人手冊), Shanghai, 1951, 556.18026/803/10085.

16. Rectify Union Organization and the Work Style of Union Cadres (Cheng-tun kung-hui tsu-chih yü kung-hui kan-pu ti kung-tso tso-feng 整頓工會組織與工會幹部的工作作風), Peking: Workers Press, 1950, 556.18/833/10106; Chao Min (趙敏), How to Run a Union Well (Tsen-

yang pan-hao kung-hui 怎樣辦好工會), Hankow, 1950, 556.18/512/10072.

17. *The Cultural Life of the Chinese Workers (Chung-kuo kung-jen ti wen-hua sheng-huo 中國工人的文化生活), Peking: Workers Press, 1955, 556.558/833/26591; Attitudes of the New Laborer (Hsin lao-tung t'ai-tu 新勞動態度), Hankow, 1950, 556.3807/813/6503.

18. The North China Communist Peasant Movement (Pei-fang kung-tang nung-min yun-tung 北方共黨農民運動), Bureau of Investigation Report, 1929, 554/4971/811/11120; Mien-yang County Committee, Propaganda Outline for Land Revolution (T'u-ti ko-ming hsuan-ch'uan ta-kang 土地革命宣傳大綱), 1931, 554.28/807/12695.

19. Southeast Shansi Peasant Union, Work Outline of the Southeast Shansi Peasant National Salvation Association (Chin-tung-nan nung-min chiu-kuo tsung-hui kung-tso kang-ling 晉東南農民救國總會工作綱領), 1939, 544.497/810/6955; Cheng Wei-san (鄭位三), The Present Situation and Peasant National Salvation Work (Mu-ch'ien chü-shih yü nung-min chiu-kuo kung-tso 目前的勢與農民救國工作), July 7th Press, no date, 544.4971/543/6770; Border Area Peasant Association, Outline on the Work of the Peasant Associations (Nung-hui kung-tso ta-kang 農會工作大綱), 1937, 544.4971/819/6862.

20. Border Area Peasant Association, Rural Village Work in the National Revolutionary United Front (Min-tsu ko-ming t'ung-i chan-hsien chung ti nung-ts'un kung-tso 民族革命統一戰線中的農村工作), no date, 544.4971/819/6860; Anti-Japanese Peasant National Salvation Association, Lectures on the Anti-Japanese Peasant Movement (K'ang-Jih nung-min yun-tung chiang-hua 抗日農民運動講話), no date, 544.4971/807/6859.

21. *Summation of the Last Year's Mass Movement in I-t'eng [Shantung] (I-t'eng i-nien lai ti ch'ün-yun tsung-chieh 嶧滕一年来的群運總結), no date, 256.2/577/3722.

22. Ch'en I (陳毅), How to Mobilize the Peasant Masses (Tsen-

yang tung-yuan nung-min ta-chung 怎樣動員農民大
眾), 1937, 544.4971/372/6712.

23. Huai-hai Peasant National Salvation Association, *The Communist Party and the Peasantry (Kung-ch'an-tang yü nung-min 共產 黨與農民), 1942, 554.497/813/6708.

24. Anhwei-Honan Border Region, Text for Workers and Peasants (Kung-nung k'o-pen 工農課本), no date, 528.4384/722/ 5320.

25. See Party Affairs, ff. 54.

26. The Communist Party and the Peasantry, p. 6.

27. See, for instance, Arthur H. Smith, Village Life in China: A Study in Sociology (New York: F. H. Revell Co., 1899).

28. CCPCC, Politburo, Chinese Communist Party's Land Policy (Chung-kuo kung-ch'an-tang ti t'u-ti cheng-ts'e 中國共產 黨的土地政策), Chi-Lu-Yü Bookstore, 1944, 554.281/ 804/13412; Hopeh-Chahar Peasant Association, Land Policy Reference Materials (T'u-ti cheng-ts'e ts'an-k'ao ts'ai-liao 土地 政策參考材料), no date, 554.281/816/6669.

29. Jo Yu (若愚), A General Summation of the Rent Reduction Movement Since the Winter of 1944 (Ssu-ssu-nien tung-chi i-lai chien-tsu yun-tung tsung-chieh 四四年冬季以來減 租運動總結), T'ai-hang District, 1945, 554.2911/ 929/6604.

30. Rent and Interest Reduction (Chien-tsu chien-hsi 減租減 息), East River Press, no date, 554.2911/838/6853.

31. Ch'en Shou-i (陳守一), et. al., A Simplified Explanation of Rent Reduction Methods (Chien-tsu pan-fa ch'ien-chieh 減 租辦法淺解), July 7th Press, 1944, 554.2911/372/6718.

32. Chi-Lu-Yü Committee, How Kuo County in Shansi Carried Out Land Reform (Shan-hsi Kuo-hsien shih tsen-yang chin-hsing t'u-ti kai-ko ti 山西崞縣是怎樣進行土地改 革的), no date, 554.28/662/6715; Liu Shao-ch'i's descrip-

tion of land reform in P'ing-shan, Hopeh was a second model;
and the third was Sui-teh, Shensi.

33. How to Organize a Force to Carry Out the Land Reform Movement (Tsen-yang tsu-chih li-liang chin-hsing t'u-ti kai-ko yun-
tung 怎樣組織力量進行土地改革運動),
New China Daily, editors, no date, 554.29/813/6925; How to
Carry Out Land Reform in the Old Liberated Areas and in the
Recently Liberated Areas (Tsai lao-ch'ü pan-lao-ch'ü tsen-yang
chin-hsing t'u-ti kai-ko 在老區半老區怎樣進
行土地改革), New China Bookstore, South Hopeh
Branch, editors, 1948, 554.29/843/6579.

"Old Liberated Areas" referred to those base areas dominated
by the Communists throughout most of the War of Resistance.
"Recently Liberated Areas" were those regions effectively con-
trolled by Communist forces after 1944.

34. Central Shantung Committee, Propaganda Bureau, Resolutely
Carry Out Land Reform and Lead the Masses to a Genuinely
New Life (Chien-chueh shih-hsing t'u-ti kai-ko ling-tao ch'ün-
chung ch'e-ti fan-shen 堅決實行土地改革領導
群眾澈底翻身), 1946, 554.29/815/6582.

35. A Record of Settling Accounts (Ch'ing-suan chi-shih 清算
紀實), Chi-Lu-Yü Bookstore, no date, 554.29/6582.

36. Land Reform Guide (T'u-ti kai-ko chih-nan 土地改革指南),
1947, 554.28/387/0204.

37. P'eng Chen (彭真), Equal Land Distribution and Rectification
Corps (P'ing-fen t'u-ti yü cheng-tun tui-wu 平分土地
與整頓隊伍), South China Press, 1948, 554.2913/397/
1056; Chin-Ch'a-Chi Military District, Political Department, Struggle to Thoroughly Eliminate Feudalism and to Equalize Land Distribution (Wei ch'e-ti hsiao-chien feng-chien p'ing-fen t'u-ti erh
tou-cheng 為澈底消滅封建平分土地而
鬥爭), 1947, 554.2913/740/6672.

38. Wu P'ing-sheng (吳平生), Study Materials on Land Reform
Laws (T'u-ti kai-ko fa hsueh-hsi tzu-liao 土地改革法
學習資料), Shanghai, 1950, 554.28/151/0143; Land

Reform Handbook (T'u-ti kai-ko shou-ts'e 土地改革
手册), Hankow, 1950, 554.28/843/0050; An Account of
the Achievement of a New Life by the Peasantry in the Suburban
Areas of Kwangtung (Kuang-tung chiao-ch'ü nung-min fan-shen
ti chi 廣東郊區農民翻身的記), Canton,
1951, 554.2931/470/0202.

39.   We are thinking of the different views expressed in Chalmers
Johnson's Peasant Nationalism and Communist Power (Stanford:
Stanford University Press, 1962); and Donald Gillin's "'Peasant
Nationalism' in the History of Chinese Communism," Journal of
Asian Studies, 23:2 (February 1964), pp. 269-289. Johnson
argues the crucial importance of anti-Japanese nationalism in
the CCP's appeal during the war while Gillin cites the Communist successes among Shansi peasants in 1936, before the war,
and their occasional apathy toward an anti-Japanese appeal later.

40.   The Bureau of Intelligence Library has some important documents
in this regard. See, Resistance University, Lecture Outline on
Class Struggle and the United Front (Chieh-chi tou-cheng yü t'ung-
i chan-hsien chiang-shou t'i-kang 階級鬥爭與統一
戰線講授提綱), no date; Guide to Mass Work
(Ch'ün-chung kung-tso chih-nan 群眾工作指南),
1945.

41.   Chin-Chi-Lu-Yü Border Government, Decision on Problems of
the Present Mass Movement (Tang-ch'ien ch'ün-chung yun-tung
wen-t'i chih chueh-ting 當前群眾運動問題之
決定), no date, 256.2/810/3711; CCPCC, Central China
Bureau, Directive on Further Arousing the Masses (Kuan-yü
chin-i-pu fa-tung ch'ün-chung ti chih-shih 關於進一步
發動群眾的指示), no date, handcopied, 256.2/
812/3724.

42.   Liu Yü-kuei (劉玉桂), Mass Work Reference Documents
(Ch'ün-chung kung-tso ts'an-k'ao wen-chien 群眾工作
參考文件), Anhwei-Kiangsu Committee, Volume II
of a two-volume set, 1943, 554.291/577/3679; Chang Lin-chih
(張霖之), et al., Mass Movement Materials (Min-yun ts'ai-
liao 民運材料), no date, 256.2/369/5721; CCPCC, Chi-
Lu-Yü Committee, Propaganda Bureau, Develop the Party in the
Mass Movement (Tsai ch'ün-chung yun-tung chung fa-chan tang

在群眾運動中發展業), 1940, 256.2/816/10259;
Fourth District Committee, *How to Arouse the Masses (Tsen-
yang fa-tung ch'ün-chung 怎樣發動群眾), no date, 256.2/
804/3714.

43. Resistance University, Education Section, Lecture Outline on the
Mass Movement (Ch'ün-chung yun-tung chiang-shou ta-kang
群眾運動講授大綱), no date, 256.2/867/10261.

44. Liu Jui-lung (劉瑞龍), Summation of the Huai-pei Area's
Five Years of Mass Work (Huai-pei wu-nien ch'ün-chung kung-tso
tsung-chieh 淮北五年群眾工作總結), 1943,
256.2/577/7264.

45. For reference to BIC holdings on internal party educational materials see our section on Party Affairs. For information on mass
work by the military see our section on Military Affairs, and
for materials on educational activities in the national salvation
associations consult the subheadings under labor, women, peasantry, etc., in this section.

46. James Pinckney Harrison, The Long March to Power (New York:
Praeger, 1972), pp. 204-206; Mark Selden, The Yenan Way in
Revolutionary China, p. 274.

47. For youth, see, Kiangsu Communist Youth League, Provincial
Committee, Provincial Committee Circular No. 1 (Sheng-wei
t'ung-kao ti-i-hao 省委通告第一號), 1930, 255.34/
806/9263; Hopei-Shansi Youth League (冀晉青聯會社), Youth
Series, (Ch'ing-nien ts'ung-shu 青年叢書), 1945?,
554.78/816/3286; for women see, Kiangnan Provincial Committee
(江南省委), Circular Number Two: Policy Line on the
Women's Movement (Sheng-wei t'ung-kao ti-erh hao: fu-nü yun-
tung ti ts'e-lueh lu hsien 省委通告第二號：婦女
運動的策略路線), 1930, 255.34/806/1250.

48. Women's Life (Fu-nü sheng-huo 婦女生活), 1932-1933,
052.9/811/16172.

49. Provincial Party Youth Committee of Western Hunan-Hupeh, Lenin
Youth (Lieh-ning ch'ing-nien 列寧青年), 1932, 052.1/812/
15572.

50. Kiangsu Communist Youth League, Vanguard (Hsien-feng 先鋒), 1933, 052.1/806.

51. "The Leadership of XX Branch in Regard to the Year End Struggle" ("XX chih-pu tui-yü nien-kuan tou-cheng ti ling-tao" X X 支部 對 於 年 關 鬥 爭 的 領導), Vanguard, #9, January 9, 1933.

52. China Women (Chung-kuo fu-nü 中國婦女), Yenan, 1939-1941, 1:1-12, 2:1-3, 7-10, 052.9/811.

53. Liu Ying (劉英), "The Broken Shoe Problem" ("P'o-hsieh wen-t'i" 破 鞋 問題), China Women, 1:2, July 1939.

54. China Youth (Chung-kuo ch'ing-nien 中國青年), 1939-1941, 1:1-9, 2:1, 3, 5, & 8-12, 3:2, 4, & 5, 052.9/803.

55. T'ung Ta-lin (童大林), "Several Types of Training for Cadres in Youth Work in North China" ("Hua-pei ch'ing-nien kung-tso kan-pu hsun-lien ti chi-chung fang-shih" 華 北 青年工作幹部訓練的幾種方式), China Youth, 2:10, October 1940.

56. John Israel, Student Nationalism in China, p. 158.

57. For an account of the youth movement and the Vanguards in North China during the War of Resistance, see, Li Ch'ang (李昌), "The Direction for Struggle of North China's Youth," ("Hua-pei ch'ing-nien tou-cheng tao-lu" 華 北青年鬥 爭道路), China Youth, 2:10, August 1940, pp. 11-23.

58. See, Our Program and Basic Atttitude (Wo-men ti kang-ling ho chi-pen t'ai-tu 我 們 的 綱領 和 基本 態度), 1937, 544.782/805/3872; Our Corps (Wo-men ti tui-wu 我 們 的 隊伍), 1936, 544.782/805/2762; Proclamation of the National Liberation Vanguards on the Present Situation (Min-tsu chieh-fang hsien-feng-tui tui shih-chü hsuan-yen 民族解 放先鋒隊對時局宣言), 1936, 544.782/805/ 17827.

59. Communist Youth League, Southern Bureau Work Committee, Propaganda Section, How to Be a Youth League Member (Tsen-

yang tso i-ko ch'ing-nien-t'uan yuan 怎樣作一個青
年團員), Hankow, 1952, 231.72/808/18831; also, Canton
Youth League, How to Establish a Communist Viewpoint on Life
(Tsen-yang chien-li kung-ch'an-chu-i jen-sheng kuan 怎樣
建立共產主義人生觀), 1952, 241.1/814/19365.

60. All China Labor Union, Women Workers Section, Handbook on
Work Among Women Workers (Nü-kung kung-tso shou-ts'e 女
工工作手冊), 1951, 556.382/803/0047.

61. Materials from the Sacrifice League, and a major Sacrifice
League Center, Hsia County, were probably captured by the
Nationalist forces of General Hu Tsung-nan who blockaded Shen-
Kan-Ning during the war. Hu's troops participated in the Shansi
New Army Incident in later 1939, when Yen Hsi-shan attempted
to liquidate the Sacrifice League's military forces, known as the
Dare-to-Die Corps or the Shansi New Army. Hsia County is in
the Southwest corner of Shansi and was within easy reach of Hu's
forces.

62. Sacrifice League, Hsia County Committee, Political Knowledge,
(Cheng-chih ch'ang-shih 政治常識), 1937, 244.3/810/
6103.

63. Sacrifice League, Hsia County Committee, Mass Movement Work
(Min-yun kung-tso 民運工作), 1939, 256.2/810/13973.

64. Sacrifice League, Hsia County Committee, Propaganda Outline
In Commemoration of the November Resolution (Shih-i-yueh chi-
nien hsuan-ch'uan t'i-kang 十一月紀念宣傳提綱),
1939, 544.784/820.

65. Sacrifice League, Justice Force (犧盟會，公道團),
Discussion Outline on Branch Problems, Organizational Life, and
Various Work Systems (Chih-pu wen-t'i tsu-chih sheng-huo chi ko-
chung kung-tso-chih t'ao-lun t'i-kang 支部問題組織生
活及各種工作制討論提綱), Hsia County,
(Third in the Organizational Problems Series), 1939, 232.5/810/
3781.

66. Po I-po (薄一波), <u>A Short History of the Sacrifice League</u> (Hsi-meng chien-shih 犧盟簡史), Hsiang-tao Press, December 1938, 544.782/631/6993.

67. The Sacrifice League's Yellow River Series includes the following: Sung Shao-wen (宋劭文), et al., <u>How We Establish Anti-Japanese Governments at the Enemies Rear</u> (Wo-men tsen-yang tsai ti-hou chien-li k'ang-Jih cheng-ch'uan 我們怎樣在 敵後建立抗日政權), May 1939, 575.2907/ 127/6022; Shih Pin (石賓), <u>A View of the Shansi Mass Movement from the Sacrifice League</u> (Ts'ung hsi-meng-hui k'an Shan-hsi min-chung yun-tung 從犧盟會看山西民眾 運動), July 1939, 544.784/65/6991; Liang Hua-chih (梁 化之), <u>United Front Work Style</u> (T'ung-i chan-hsien ti tso-feng 統一戰線的作風), August 1939, 295/336/3056.

68. Dare-to-Die Corps, 10th Column, <u>Sentinel</u> (Ch'ien-shao 前哨), #3, 4, 7, 12, no date, 052.4/737.

III.   CULTURAL AND EDUCATIONAL AFFAIRS

One of the most enduring themes in Chinese Communist thought
and practice is the commitment to the transformation of China's traditional culture.   Whereas Lenin postponed the "Cultural Revolution"
in Russian society until after the seizure of political power,[1] the
Chinese elite confronted the difficult task of cultural change in the
process of the revolutionary struggle.   Indeed, following the May
Fourth Movement of 1919 and, more generally, under the influence
of the New Culture Movement of 1917-1922, the CCP from its establishment in 1921 has been intimately involved with the revolution in
China's literature and art and the reformation of the educational system.[2]   This is reflected in the Bureau's impressive collection of
novels and plays, and of CCP decisions regarding the arts and education from the late 1920s to the early 1950s.

A.   Literature and Art

The modern Chinese literary tradition is marked by the movement for colloquial literature in the 1920s, and by the polemics among
leftist writers over the nature of revolutionary literature and national
defense literature in the 1930s.[3]   The journals of the Romantic-turned-
Marxist Creation Society (1921-1929), Sun Society (1927-1929), and the
League of Left Wing Writers (1930-1936) were major publications for
leftist and Communist statements on the nature of the literary movement.[4]   As part of the struggle to develop a genuine literature of and
for the masses, some attempts were made within the Communist underground cells of Shanghai and the Red Army in the Soviets to utilize
the arts for purposes of mass mobilization and political indoctrination.
The BIC has some materials from these early experiments with socialist realism and mass art.   These include, for example, a 1932
play entitled A Brothers' Quarrel (Jan chi chu-tou), used by the Red
Army in the Kiangsi Soviet,[5] and a collection of revolutionary songs
published by the East Hupeh Action Committee.[6]   There is also a
Party periodical, Youth Life (Ch'ing-nien sheng-huo), printed in
Shanghai which included short stories and poems laden with Marxist
themes.[7]

When the war with Japan broke out in 1937, polemics on national
defense literature ended abruptly.   Prominent leftist artists gathered in

Hankow in 1938 and united to form the All China Anti-Aggression
Federation of Writers and Artists (Chung-hua ch'üan-kuo wen-i-chieh
k'ang-ti hsieh-hui) to undertake wartime propaganda work at the front
lines. 8   Indeed, before the Federation was created, many students
and writers had traveled to Yenan or had gone to the front and joined
the Communist Eighth Route Army.   In the early war years cultural
work in conjunction with mass mobilization was neither systematic
nor uniform.   The leading literary critics continued to polemicize
standards for mass literature and the question of a "national form"
(min-tsu hsing-shih), while the cultural workers in the Communist
base areas experimented with plays and traditional folk art in their
efforts to enlist mass support for the resistance.   The best general
survey of Communist cultural activities and work in this period is
an article by Ho Lo. 9   In this survey he discusses the principal
plays, short stories, and novels of those years as well as the village
arts drive in the Shen-Nan-King and Chin-Ch'a-Chi Border Region.

Ho's essay appears in the Cultural Brigade (Wen-hua tsung-tui),
an important theoretical journal and the voice of North China Unified
University (Hua-pei Lien-ta), which was a cadre training school formed
from the merger of four Yenan schools and which moved to the front
in 1939. 10   Cultural Brigade was a forerunner of the academic journals prominent in the People's Republic after 1949, such as the
Chinese People's University's Education and Research (Chiao-yü yü
yen-chiu); it includes articles on educational methodology, the workers'
and women's movements, and cadre work style.   Each edition contains
art work, songs, and poetry.

There were several other important Communist literary journals
published at this time in Yenan, of which the BIC has partial runs.
Mass Literature and Art (Ta-chung wen-i), the namesake of an earlier
publication from the League of Left Wing Writers era, was an influ-
ential forum in which Mao Tun, Chou Wen, Ting Ling, and other
writers expressed their views on a number of literary problems. 11
A typical issue contains two or three topical articles, plus short
stories and poetry dealing with patriotic themes.   There are also
essays of the tsa-wen genre in which, for example, Chou Wen discusses differences between creative and collective life and Ting Ling
comments on the relationship between the writer and the masses. 12
Certain editions deal with special topics such as the Bolshevik Revolution and the drama movement.

China Culture (Chung-kuo wen-hua) and Literature and Art Battle-line (Wen-i chan-hsien) were two of the most significant literary magazines printed in Yenan.[13] Their articles on "national form" shaped what became the orthodox Communist viewpoint on the subject.[14] In addition, the inaugural issue of China Culture includes Mao Tse-tung's important essay on New Democracy, which appears to have been written specifically for this edition.[15] In comparison to Mass Literature and Art, however, these journals have less to do with actual literature and more with literary theory.

Theatrical presentations were a major form of propaganda and mass mobilization during the war. The Bureau holds several plays from this period, including a few performed by Ting Ling's Front Service Group.[16] In addition, there are also plays used by the New Fourth Army in Central China,[17] plus several novels,[18] and an important discussion of the drama movement led by the CCP.[19]

The general direction of CCP cultural policy during the war was towards the creation of mass cultural forms, although there often was a reliance on traditional modes such as folk opera or harvest dances. This movement not only provided, in the words of Mao Tun, "new wine for old bottles,"[20] but also was a serious attempt to state the resistance motif in a form easily recognizable by the peasantry. Many of the ideas from the old controversy on "national form" were revived in the search for a basis of the new mass literature. Indeed, much of this experience was reflected in Mao Tse-tung's speech on literature and art in May 1942, which enunciated the policy of a literature for the workers, peasants, and soldiers and set the standards for future mass cultural activities.

Mao's speech also initiated the village arts movement in which the CCP encouraged the production of village plays and drama. Plays in the BIC present many of the resistance themes used in this movement, such as joining the army,[21] fighting the Japanese,[22] self-defense forces,[23] examining road passes,[24] character study,[25] reclaiming waste lands and production,[26] and cowherds.[27] Among the plays is The White-haired Girl, a perennially popular play which was rewritten in the Cultural Revolution.[28] The BIC also holds Yuan Ching's Rent Reduction (Chien-tsu), a harvest song play and part of the Pao-an Drama Troupe's repertoire which was based on the rent reduction drive in the Shen-Kan-Ning Border Region in the early 1940s.[29] The villain of the story is a recalcitrant landlord, "Two-

Road" Mao-tzu, who feared public censure yet secretly pressed his tenants to continue paying old rent rates while he publicly proclaimed reductions. Another central character is one of his tenants, Pai Kuei. Far from an ideal hero, he is quite spineless. Indeed, Pai stands up to the landlord only because of the prodding of his wife, Pai Ch'i, an activist in the local women's movement. Other characters include a local activist tenant and a border government official who both push for rent reduction in the village.

Another significant play from the War of Resistance and one recently revived in the post-Cultural Revolution period is Yao Chung-ming's, Comrade, You've Taken the Wrong Path! (T'ung-chih, ni tsou ts'o-le lu!).[30] The author, a diplomat in later years, based the play on his experience with the Eighth Route Army in Shantung. The plot is not so important as the author's introduction in which he describes how mass criticism aided his writing. The war provided Yao his first contact with the world of the common people and, to make the play believeable to the peasantry, he solicited the opinions of older cadres, villagers, and soldiers on the proper language, dialogue, and plot, making significant changes through mutual criticism and self-criticism. Chou Yang's preface to the play is also an important source on Chinese Communist theories of mass literature and art.

The most significant play from the war period held by the BIC is the Song of the Poor (Ch'iung-jen lo), the model play of the village art and literature movement in 1944.[31] In original form, it had no script but was a series of improvisations on the life of the peasants of High Street Village in Fu-p'ing, Hopeh. The actors were the villagers themselves, reenacting the drama of the war. The first scene was set in 1928, the year a great flood wracked Fu-p'ing, and it was used to set up a contrast between the old life under the Nationalists and the warlords with the new life which began with the arrival of the Eighth Route Army in 1937. Subsequent scenes concerned combat with the Japanese, production work, mutual aid, and other activities typical of the Communist wartime programs. Local cadres eventually wrote a script and added a song by one of the border region's leading cultural workers. But the significance of the play remained its depiction of social change and the villagers' vicarious participation in a type of dramatic catharsis which freed them from the bonds of traditional society.

Another major art form of the War of Resistance was the harvest song (yang-ko), which was part of the traditional music lore of North

China.[32]   In 1941 students at the North China Unified University de-
bated the use of such harvest songs in the village arts movement, but
the propagandistic utility of this traditional art form remained undecided.
Plays such as Rent Reduction often incorporated the harvest song into
the presentation but some drama troupes used the songs only in
dances.[33]   Other cadres specialized in collecting and preserving popular melodies and adapting for wartime propaganda.   One such collection available at the BIC, edited by the Popular Music Study Group,
includes some ninety-one tunes, primarily from the Sui-teh and Mi-
chih Districts in Shensi.[34]   Most of the melodies in the collection
are in the traditional five tone arrangement, and for some, editors
have added new lyrics to the score.

The Civil War in China brought little change in Communist cultural policy.   Plays such as Earthquake (Ti-chen) written in 1946 continued to emphasize the transformation of the peasants' lives--in this
case the changing of land relationships between 1933 and 1943 in
southern Shantung.[35]   Many of the Bureau's materials from this period
come from Shantung, and the BIC has several issues of the Shantung
Federation of Cultural Workers publication, Cultural Transformation
(Wen-hua fan-shen).[36]   There also are other interesting literary
publications from the Civil War in the BIC, such as the Literature
and Art Magazine (Wen-i tsa-chih), a journal devoted primarily to
cultural activities related to land reform,[37] plus several issues of
North China Culture (Pei-fang wen-hua), a bi-weekly published in
Kalgan.[38]   The latter was under the direction of Ch'eng Fang-wu and
the dramatist Sha K'o-fu, and had an impressive editorial board of
Chou Yang, Teng T'o, Ai Ch'ing, and others.   The content of the
magazine was varied.   Hsiao Chün, the noted Manchurian novelist,
for instance, contributed an article on Northeast China in a March
issue, while the following edition had a play by Ting Ling entitled
Looking Homeward (Wang-hsiang-t'ai).   Finally, there are handbooks
and other documents used by cadres in cultural work from this period.[39]

The BIC's materials on literature and art after the Communist
victory in the Civil War are limited.   The new regime's continued
emphasis on revolutionary literature, portraying heroic workers and
the bitter experiences of the masses in China before 1949 is reflected
in the archive's holdings.[40]   There are also a few novels from after
1949, though generally the Bureau's collection in this area is not so
good as those in many Western libraries with holdings on contemporary
China.   There are some items, such as Thought Magazine (Ssu-hsiang

tsa-chih), which would provide information on cultural activities and Communist programs of thought reform in the intellectual community.[41]

B. Education

Party educational activities were directly related to cultural programs. In the War of Resistance, for example, the Communists linked the village art movement with political education work. The BIC has an unusual collection of social education primers, school texts, and periodicals dating from 1937 to around 1958. Adult education programs were widely promoted in the Communist base areas, and the BIC has a number of character study primers[42] and "winter-study movement" texts[43] from Shen-Kan-Ning, Shantung, Huai-pei and other areas. There is also an almost complete collection of primary school materials used in Yenan. These include a series of history and geography texts edited by Hsin An-t'ing for both the primary and middle school levels.[44] In addition, there are mathematics texts,[45] natural science books,[46] and a seven-volume language primer complied by Tung Ch'un-ts'ai.[47] Finally, there are texts from other base areas such as five volumes of an eight-volume language set from Chin-Ch'a-Chi.[48]

These materials are valuable references on the Communist viewpoint towards Chinese history, science, and the general world order. Furthermore, at the beginning of the war the Communists called for a general reform of educational curricula, and textbooks in the BIC-- particularly the Chinese (kuo-yü) primers--reflect this reform, as well as present some of the social and political themes of the New Democracy.

The Bureau also has a number of post-1949 school texts. These include kindergarten primers as well as history, science, and foreign language books for middle schools.[49] The BIC holds several education journals from the mid-1940s.[50] The most important of these is Education Frontline (Chiao-yü chen-ti), a publication of the Chin-Ch'a-Chi Border Region Education Office.[51] Several issues of this periodical are available in the United States, but the Bureau holds some unavailable outside of mainland China. This is the only journal we know of in which the Communists discuss the theory and practice of the popular education movement (1943-1945). Many of the articles are by leading educational figures in Yenan and Chin-Ch'a-Chi, such as Liu K'ai-feng and Tung Ch'un-ts'ai.

Finally, there are materials in the BIC on the New Enlightenment Movement (1936-1937) initiated by Ch'en Po-ta. The central theme of this united front type philosophical movement was the search for the unity of the "new philosophy" (i.e., Marxism-Leninism) with the concrete reality of China. Documents, such as Ai Ssu-ch'i's _A History of the Modern Chinese Enlightenment Movement_, detail Ch'en's role in this movement which was terminated prematurely by the Japanese invasion.[52]

FOOTNOTES TO CHAPTER III

1. Alfred G. Meyer, Leninism, (New York: Praeger, 1967), pp. 213-215.

2. Chow Tse-tsung, The May Fourth Movement: Intellectual Revolution in Modern China (Stanford: Stanford University Press, 1960).

3. The 1927-1929 debate on revolutionary literature generated more heat than light and was complicated by factionalism. On the extreme left the Creation and Sun Societies quarrelled with each other while joining first in attacks on moderate leftists like Mao Tun, Lu Hsun, and their affiliates on the Threads-of-Talk (Yü-ssu), and second in sallies against the Anglo-American liberalism of the Crescent Moon group. In the spring of 1930 the extreme left and the moderate left joined in the formation of the League of Left Wing Writers. This Communist-led group existed precariously above and below ground until the spring of 1936 when, in line with the new United Front policy of the CCP, it was dissolved by the Chou Yang faction of the League in favor of a more open and inclusive organization promoting "national defense literature." Lu Hsun, long at odds with Chou Yang, proposed a counter slogan of "mass literature of the national revolutionary struggle" through his associate Hu Feng. The conflict between the two groups was intense in mid-1936, but diminished with the death of Lu Hsun in October 1936 and the outbreak of the Sino-Japanese War in July 1937. (We would like to thank Harriet C. Mills for her preparation of this footnote.)

4. Amitendranath Tagore, Literary Debates in Modern China, 1918-1937 (Tokyo: Center for Far East Asian Culture, 1967).

5. Red Army, General Political Department, A Brothers' Quarrel (Jan chi chu-tou 燃箕煮荳), 1932, 654.91/811/11451.

6. East Hupeh Action Committee, Collection of Revolutionary Songs (Ko-ming ko-chi 革命歌集), 1930, 649.3/812/21714.

7. Youth Life (Ch'ing-nien sheng-huo 青年生活), Shanghai, 1930, 052.9/805/16189.

8. The Center for Chinese Research Materials in Washington, D.C. has printed the organ of this federation, K'ang-chan wen-i (Literature of the War of Resistance) in four volumes, covering the original ten volumes (with missing issues) published between 1938 and 1946.

9. Ho Lo (何洛), "A General View of the Culture and Literature Movement in the Last Four Years in the North China Anti-Japanese Bases" ("Ssu-nien lai Hua-pei k'ang-Jih ken-chü-ti ti wen-i yun-tung kai-kuan" 四年來華北抗日根據地的文藝運動概觀), Cultural Brigade (Wen-hua tsung-tui 文化縱隊), #2:1, July 1941, pp. 7-10, 30-32.

10. North China Unified University, Cultural Brigade (Wen-hua tsung-tui 文化縱隊), 1940-1941, #1:4-6, 2:1, 4, 052.51/878/16157 and 525.689/872/5605; See also, North China Unified University Life (Lien-ta sheng-huo 聯大生活), 1940-1941, #3, 7, 8, 14, 15, 052.51/878.

The four schools merged into North China Unified University were the North Shensi Public School, the Lu Hsun Academy, the Workers School, and the Youth Training Institute. In 1945 the school was moved to Kalgan and became the North China People's University.

11. All China Anti-Aggression Federation of Writers and Artists, Mass Literature and Art (Ta-chung wen-i 大眾文藝), 1939-1940, 1:2, 3, 5, 6, 2:1, 2, 3, 052.5/803.

12. Tsa-wen is a short essay on a variety of topics often used for social commentary.

13. China Culture (Chung-kuo wen-hua 中國文化), Yenan, 1940, 1:1, 6, 2:1-4, 052.5/804; Literature and Art Battleline (Wen-i chan-hsien 文藝戰線), Yenan, Life Bookstore, 1939, (Chou Yang, editor), #2 and 3, 052.5/808.

14. For a complete collection of all of the essays on "national form" see Hu Feng (胡風), *Collection on the National Form Debate (Min-tsu hsing-shih t'ao-lun chi 民族形式討論集), Chungking, 1941, 546.59/236/1828.

62

15. *Mao Tse-tung, A New Democratic Politics and a New Democratic Culture (Hsin-min-chu-chu-i ti cheng-chih yü hsin-min-chu-chu-i ti wen-hua 新民主主義的政治與新民主主義的文化). See China Culture, 1:1, February 15, 1940, pp. 2-24.

16. Masses Drama Society (大眾劇社), Smash the Devils (Ta kuei-tzu ch'ü 打鬼子去), 1941, 654.91/803/6359.

17. New Fourth Army, Fifth Division, Political Department, Pigs Bearing Arms (Ch'ün-chu shih-ch'iang 蠢豬拖槍), 1942, no BIC number.

18. Chang Keng (張庚), Going Home (Ta hui lao-chia ch'ü 打回老家去), Drama Press, 1938, 654.91/369/5758; Liu Pai-yü (劉白羽), Beneath the Wu-t'ai Mountains (Wu-t'ai-shan hsia 五台山下), Chungking: Life Press, 1939, 657.96/577/5665.

19. Cheng Chun-li (鄭君里), On the Resistance War Drama Movement (Lun k'ang-chan hsi-chu yun-tung 論抗戰戲劇運動), Chungking: Life Press, 1939, 654.9/543/3696.

20. Mao Tun (茅盾), "Old Form, Popular Form, and National Form" ("Chiu hsing-shih, min-chien hsing-shih yü min-tsu hsing-shih" 舊性式, 民間性式與民族性式), China Culture (Chung-kuo wen-hua 中國文化), 2:1, September 1940, 052.5/804.

21. Sun Hung (孫洪), Second Brother Chang Joins the Army (Chang erh ko ts'an-chün 張二哥參軍), Chi-Lu-Yü Bookstore, 1946, 654.9/330/6057.

22. 120th Division, Propaganda Department, Niu Yung-kuei is Wounded (Niu Yung-kuei shou-shang 牛永貴受傷), 1944, 654.9/810/5422.

23. Shantung Writers Federation, Self-Defense (Tzu-wei 自衛), no date, 654.9/945/6269.

24. Ma Chien-ling (馬健翎), Inspect the Road Passes (Ch'a lu-t'iao 查路條), Chi-Lu-Yü Bookstore, no date, 654.9/294/6078.

25. Ma K'o (馬可), <u>The Couple Learns to Read</u> (<u>Fu-ch'i shih-tzu</u> 夫妻識字), 1945, 654.9/294/6388.

26. <u>Reclaiming the Waste Land</u> (<u>Ta-huang pien-le</u> 大荒變了), Popular Literature and Art Press, 1944, 654.9/933/5554.

27. Chang Tzu-li (張自力), <u>The New Little Cowherd</u> (<u>Hsin hsiao-</u> <u>fang-niu</u> 新小放牛), no date, 654.9/369/6068.

28. July Drama Society (七月劇社), <u>The White-haired Girl</u> (<u>Pai-</u> <u>mao-nü ch'uan-p'u</u> 白毛女全譜), no date, 654.95/802/ 5762; also, Federation of Shantung Cultural Workers, <u>Collection</u> <u>of Village Drama Troupe Productions</u> (<u>Nung-ts'un chü-t'uan</u> <u>ch'uang-tso hsuan-chi</u> 農村劇團創作選集), New China Bookstore, 1946, 654.91/804/6764.

29. Yuan Ching (袁靜), <u>Rent Reduction</u> (<u>Chien-tsu</u> 減租), Yenan, North China Bookstore, no date, 654.91/297/6593.

30. Yao Chung-ming (姚仲明), <u>Comrade, You've Taken the</u> <u>Wrong Path!</u> (<u>T'ung-chih, ni tsou ts'o-le lu</u>! 同志,你 走錯了路), Su-pei Press, 1945, 649/265/6046.

31. High Street Village Drama Troupe (高街村劇團), <u>Song</u> <u>of the Poor</u> (<u>Ch'iung-jen lo</u> 窮人樂), Masses Bookstore, 1946, 654.91/810/6962.

32. Harvest songs, or a more accurate translation being "rice-sprout" songs, were originally sung by the peasants of North China while transplanting rice seedlings. When the Communists moved into these regions they quickly adopted the songs as part of their propaganda, infusing them with political and patriotic themes. Indeed, harvest songs represented the Communist's first effort at combining propaganda and entertainment and were the forerunner of the revolutionary ballets and plays, such as the recently popular <u>Red Detachment of Women</u>.

33. China Popular Music Study Group (中國民間音樂研究會), editor, <u>Harvest Song Selection</u> (<u>Yang-ko ch'ü-hsuan</u> 秧歌曲選), New China Bookstore, 1944, 653.8/843/6264. There are four songs from the Chin-Sui Border Region and a few more from Lung-tung (隴東), San-pien (三邊), Mi-chih (米脂), and Sui-teh (綏德) districts in Shensi.

CCP district organizations in the Shen-Kan-Ning Border Region were often named after a prominent county (hsien) located in the district. Thus, there are documents in the BIC from both the Sui-teh and Mi-chih county and district organizations of the CCP. Other districts were often given a name which was a combination of two characters, each taken from a separate county in the district. Still other districts, particularly in the Chin-Chi-Lu-Yü and Chin-Ch'a-Chi Border Regions were referred to by numbers, although this practice was often used in addition to given names.

34. *Selection of Harvest Song Plays (Yang-ko chu hsuan-chi 秧歌劇選集), 1947, 736.16/396/5676.

35. Chia Chi (賈霽), Earthquake (Ti-chen 地震), 1946, no BIC number.

36. Cultural Transformation (Wen-hua fan-shen 文化翻身), no date, 052.5/804/5608.

37. Literature and Art Magazine (Wen-i tsa-chih 文藝雜誌), 1946, 1:3-5, 3:4, 4:1, 052.4/804.

38. North China Culture (Pei-fang wen-hua 北方文化), Kalgan, 1946, 1:1-3, 6, 2:1, 052.5/805.

39. K'ai Feng (凱豐), Cultural Readers (Wen-hua k'o-pen 文化課本), 1944, 244.3/942/4938.

40. Collection of Literary Creations by Shanghai Workers (Shang-hai kung-jen wen-i ch'uang-tso hsuan-chi 上海工人文藝創作選集), Shanghai, 1956, 649/843/30633. Similar materials are available at the Harvard-Yenching Library, Cambridge, Massachusetts.

41. *Thought Magazine (Ssu-hsiang tsa-chih 思想雜誌), Wuhan, 1950-1953, 520.23/204; the BIC has a more complete collection of this periodical than available in U.S. libraries; also, Kwangtung People's Government Education Office, Study Materials for the Thought Reform of University Teachers (Kao-teng hsueh-hsiao chiao-shih ssu-hsiang kai-tsao hsueh-hsi tzu-liao 高等學校教師思想改造學習資料), 1952, 520.25/724/19317-8.

42. Shen-Kan-Ning Border Region, Education Office, Tung Ch'un-ts'ai (董純才), editor, New One-thousand Character Text (Hsin ch'ien tzu wen 新千字文), no date, 528.4384/478/5096; Shen-Kan-Ning Border Region, Education Office, Liu Yü (劉御), Literacy Primer (Shih-tzu k'o-pen 識字課本), 1938, 528.4384/577/5279.

43. Shantung Administrative Office, Winter Study Political Text (Tung-hsueh cheng-chih k'o-pen 冬學政治課本), no date, 528.4384/713/7148; T'ai-hang Administrative Office, Winter Study Current Events Reader (Tung-hsueh shih-shih tu-pen 冬學 時事讀本), Masses Bookstore, 1946, 528.4384/718/5709; Huai-pei Administrative Office, Talks on Winter Study (Tung-hsueh chiang-hua 冬學講話), 1944, 528.7384/721/5173.

44. Shen-Kan-Ning Border Region, Hsin An-t'ing (辛安亭), History Text (Li-shih k'o-pen 歷史課本), 1939, 3 volumes, 523.841/135/5147; Shen-Kan-Ning Border Region, Geography Text (Ti-li k'o-pen 地理課本), 1939, 523.841/135/5148.

45. Chu Kuang (朱光), Mathematics Text (Suan-shu k'o-pen 算術課本), Yenan: North China Bookstore, 1942, 523.841/114/5141.

46. Wen Chi-tzu (温濟澤), Natural Science Text (Tzu-jan k'o-hsueh k'o-pen 自然科學課本), Yenan: North China Bookstore, 1942, 523.841/456/5157.

47. Shen-Kan-Ning Border Region, Tung Ch'un-ts'ai (董純才), Chinese Text (Kuo-yü k'o-pen 國語課本), 7 volumes, no date, 523.841/810.

48. Chin-Ch'a-Chi Border Region, Education Office, editors, Chinese Text (Kuo-yü k'o-pen 國語課本), Volumes 1-4, 7, 1945, 523.841/810/5303; Other Border Region materials include Hung Lin (洪林), Chinese Text (Kuo-yü k'o-pen 國語課本), Central Shantung Daily Press, 1944, 523.841/226/5396.

49. Shen Pai-ying (沈白英), New Text for Kindergarten (Yu-chih-yuan hsin k'o-pen 幼稚園新課本), Shanghai: Commercial Press, 1951, 523.285/128/26232; North China Unified University, History Research Office, Modern Chinese History

(Chung-kuo chin-tai-shih 中 國 近 代 史), Shanghai: New
China Press, 1949, 524.831/872/18933; Shanghai Bookstore,
Chemistry (Hua-hsueh 化學), Shanghai, 1957, 524.8313/833/
37964; Harbin Foreign Language Institute, editor, Russian Reader
(O-yü tu-pen 俄 語 讀 本), Peking: Modern Press, 1956,
524.831/869/35104.

50. Chin-Ch'a-Chi Border Region, Education Office, Border Area
Education (Pien-ch'ü chiao-yü 邊 區 教 育), 1939-1941,
052.51/720; Central Kiangsu Education (Su-chung chiao-yü
蘇 中 教 育), 1945, #4, 6-9, 052.1/820.

51. Education Frontline (Chiao-yü chen-ti 教 育 陣 地), Fu-p'ing
and Kalgan, 1944-1947, 2:5, 6, 4:4, 5:3, 5; 052.51/811; (Hoover
has 5:6, 6:1-3, 7:1, 2.)

52. Ai Ssu-ch'i, A History of the Modern Chinese Enlightenment Movement (Chin-tai chung-kuo ch'i-meng yun-tung shih 近 代 中
國 啓 蒙 運 動 史), Shanghai: Life Bookstore, 1938, no
BIC number.

IV. MILITARY AFFAIRS

The BIC has an impressive collection of materials on Communist military affairs. The heaviest concentration is from the War of Resistance (1937-1945), but apparently there are also a number of uncatalogued documents from the Kiangsi Soviet (1931-1934).[1] Included are reports on strategy and tactics and on political work in the army along with the circulars and military journals of individual units. The most important single source is the BIC's run of thirty-three issues of the Eighth Route Army's Military and Political Journal (Chün-cheng tsa-chih).[2] In addition, scattered materials are available on the People's Liberation Army after 1949, along with a number of Nationalist intelligence reports on Communist military affairs compiled by the Bureau.

Numerous articles and manuals on military strategy and tactics from the War of Resistance provide materials for a comparison between Mao Tse-tung's theories on guerrilla warfare and those of the Soviet-trained high command. According to William Whitson, the high command supported more conventional warfare,[3] and it appears that some top generals disagreed with Mao on the speed of the regularization of militia units and the scope of mobile warfare.[4] Several manuals on guerrilla strategy and tactics written at the beginning of the war with Japan by Communist leaders such as P'eng Hsueh-feng, Chang Tso-hua, and Fan Wen-lan treat these issues.[5]

The BIC also has many tracts on political work in the army during the War of Resistance. These include a collection of articles edited by Li Fu-ch'un and a volume written by Chang Tso-hua.[6] The emphasis in the military was on mass mobilization, unit consolidation, political indoctrination, and enemy troop work. The Bureau holds several documents on mass mobilization by the army[7] and an even larger collection of materials on unit consolidation, which emphasize company level political work and improved relations between officers and enlisted men.[8] There are also many directives, manuals, work plans, and circulars which touch on political operations within the Army's ranks.[9] Researchers interested in military work may also consult the Bureau of Intelligence Library, which has a great number of documents and periodicals on military affairs--especially company political work--dating from 1942 to 1947 from Shantung. The Soldiers' Monthly (Chan-shih yueh-k'an), for example, includes a number of

67

significant articles by Hsiao Hua, Lo Jung-huan, and Li Yu on the problems of company political work before and after the Rectification Drive (1942-1944).[10]

The Rectification Drive had a significant impact on the military, particularly after the Northwest Bureau Senior Cadre Conference in January 1943. There are several documents from that conference relating to military affairs which are in the BIC, including Ho Lung's report on the rectification of the military and Jen Pi-shih's speech which called for the elimination of tendencies toward warlordism within the army.[11] After the conference T'an Cheng gave two important speeches at a military cadre conference in Yenan in January 1943 and April 1944 on the rectification campaign in the military, both of which are in the BIC.[12] In the army, moreover, the Rectification Drive spawned several other drives such as the "Cherish the People, Support the Government" movement, a military production drive, and a renewed emphasis on unit solidarity; certain aspects of these drives are documented in the Bureau.[13]

The BIC holdings of the Military and Political Journal are the most extensive we know of outside mainland China. The Eighteenth Group Army Political Department published this periodical monthly from January 1939 to sometime in 1942. It includes articles by all the major military figures of that time, including many who have been active in Chinese politics since 1949.[14] A typical issue has around one hundred pages and includes from six to ten articles on a variety of major subjects, such as cadre education and the development of base areas. In addition, there are translations from Russian on Marxist theory and from Japanese on military tactics, obituaries of fallen heroes, and war reports. As an example of an ordinary issue's content, the June 1940 edition includes articles by P'eng Teh-huai on China's national crisis, Ch'en Man-yuan on repelling the Japanese offensive in West Hopeh that year, Chang Ch'ih-min on the Army's initial activities in the Chi-Lu-Yü Base Area, Chou Shih-ti on the 120th Division's campaign in Central Hopeh, and T'ien Fu on political and military education for "cadres in service" (tsai-chih kan-pu). There is also a special collection of five articles on "enemy work" which consisted of instruction in Japanese language and the interrogation of Japanese prisoners. Not all of the articles in the Military and Political Journal concern North China, and there are a good number of accounts of the New Fourth Army's activities in Central China.

The Bureau has a number of intelligence reports from Nationalist agencies on the Communist military. Some are available in Western and Japanese libraries, but others are classified "secret." They range from battlefield accounts with maps and charts to analyses of internal power struggles in the Red Army.[15] These reports naturally reflect an adversary's viewpoint, but are valuable in giving another perspective on Communist military operations. For example, Personal Relations and Factional Struggle Among the Communist Bandits, although undocumented and based in part on rumor, is suggestive of factional divisions within the army and demonstrates one approach to understanding Chinese Communist military activities.[16]

Finally, the BIC has scattered materials from the People's Liberation Army after 1949. These include such recent documents as the newspaper, National Defense Fighters (Kuo-fang chan-shih), published in 1972 by the Kunming Military District Political Department with articles concerning political work at the company level and problems of work style.[17] Unfortunately, military materials from the period after 1949 are generally not listed in the card catalogue and it is difficult to assess the range and scope of the Bureau holdings for this period.

FOOTNOTES TO CHAPTER IV

1. For a critique of the North China Soviet strategy by Chang Wen-t'ien, see Lo Fu (洛甫), A Criticism of Mistakes in Guerrilla Warfare in Hopeh's Kao-yang and Li Counties (Kuan-yü Ho-pei Kao-yang Li hsien yu-chi chan-cheng ti ts'o-wu ti p'i-p'ing 關於河北高陽蠡縣游擊戰爭的錯誤的批評), 1932, 592.941/939/17775.

2. Eighteenth Group Army, General Political Department, Military and Political Journal (Chün-cheng tsa-chih 軍政雜誌), 1:1-12, 2:1-12, 3:1, 3, 7 and 10, 4:1-3, 052.4/732. 4:1 has an index to Volume 3. There are only four issues of this periodical in the U.S. and Japan.

3. William Whitson and Huang Chen-hsia in The Chinese High Command, argue that there was a major confrontation between Mao and many of the Communist generals over tactics and strategy during the War of Resistance. Many of Mao's military writings are available at the BIC, but these are just as readily available in the Selected Military Writings of Mao Tse-tung (Peking: Foreign Language Press, 1963). The Eighth Route Army Military and Political Journal often discusses tactical problems and might be used to contrast opposing viewpoints on these questions. See specifically, Liu Po-ch'eng, "On Guerrilla Warfare and Mobile Warfare" ("Lun yu-chi chan yü yun-tung chan" 論游擊戰與運動戰), 1:4, April 1939. Also, there are some manuals on tactics. See, for example, Forward Army (挺進大隊), Political Department, Tactics of War (Chan-shu kai-tse 戰術概則), no date, 592.94/810/4310.

4. P'eng Teh-huai discussed these problems in a report to the T'ai-hang Senior Cadre Conference in December 1942 (cited in Party Affairs, ff. 54). Again the Military and Political Journal is an important source. See, for example, Shu T'ung (舍同), "Political Work in the Chin-Ch'a-Chi Military District During the Last Three Years of the War of Resistance" ("Chin-Ch'a-Chi chün-ch'ü k'ang-chan san-nien lai ti cheng-chih kung-tso" 晉察冀軍區抗戰三年來的政治工作), 2:11, November 1940.

5. P'eng Hsueh-feng (彭雪楓), <u>Several Basic Principles of War in Guerrilla Tactics</u> (Yu-chi chan-shu ti chi-ko chi-pen tso-chan yuan-tse 游擊戰術的幾個基本作戰原則), 1939, 592.941/397/4263; Chang Tso-hua (張佐華), <u>Discussions on Guerrilla Tactics</u> (Yu-chi chan-shu chiang-hua 游擊戰術講話), Life Bookstore, 1938, 592.941; Fan Wen-lan (范文瀾), <u>Guerrilla Tactics</u> (Yu-chi chan-shu 游擊戰術), 1937, 592.941/398.

6. Li Fu-ch'un (李富春), editor, <u>The War of Resistance and the Political Tasks in the Army</u> (K'ang-chan yü chün-tui cheng-chih kung-tso 抗戰與軍隊政治工作), Hankow: Life Bookstore, 1938, 596.872/144/4336; Chang Tso-hua (張佐華), <u>The Political Work of Resistance Armies</u> (K'ang-chan chün-tui ti cheng-chih kung-tso 抗戰軍隊的政治工作), Hankow, 1938, 596.872/369/4424.

7. Hopeh-Chahar Guerrilla Command (冀察游擊司令部), <u>Mass Movement</u> (Min-chung yun-tung 民眾運動), 1938?, 540.931/746/3688.

8. Eighteenth Group Army, Political Department, <u>Company Work</u>, (Lien-tui kung-tso 連隊工作), 1946, 590.856/732/4354; New Fourth Army, Political Department, <u>Initial Research on Company Work</u> (Lien-tui kung-tso ch'u-pu yen-chiu 連隊工作初步研究), 1942, 590.856/743/4473; Eighth Route Army, Political Department, <u>Political Work Regulations</u> (Cheng-chih kung-tso t'iao-li 政治工作條例), 1939?, 596.872/732/4381; P'eng Hsueh-feng, <u>Course on Guerrilla Unit Political Work</u> (Yu-chi-tui cheng-chih kung-tso chiao-ch'eng 游擊隊政治工作教程), Yenan: Liberation Press, 1938, 596.872/392/4445.

9. New Fourth Army, Seventh Division, Political Department, <u>Directives on Military Affairs</u> (Chün-shih chih-shih 軍事指示), 1947, 590.8/735/11884; New Fourth Army, <u>Military Affairs Notification</u> (Chün-shih t'ung-chih 軍事通知), 1945, 590.8/745/4894; Central Hopeh Military District, Second Sub-district, Political Department, <u>Outline of Company Political Work</u> (Lien-tui cheng-chih kung-tso t'i-kang 連隊政治工作提綱), August 1938, 590.82/746/4341; Hsing-t'ang County, Military Committee (行唐縣武委會),

Political Text (Cheng-chih k'o-pen 政治課本), April 1945, 593.824/806/4493.

10. 115th Division, Political Department, <u>Soldiers' Monthly</u> (<u>Chan-shih yueh-k'an</u> 戰士月刊), #2, 3, 5, 9, 15, 55 and 59. See April 1942 edition (#2) on Company Political Work and the special issue of May 1944; also of value is the New Fourth Army, Shantung Military District, <u>Military and Political Fortnightly</u> (<u>Chün-cheng pan-yueh-k'an</u> 軍政半月刊), 1946-1947, #2, 3, 4, 6, 9, and 11.

11. For Ho Lung's report see, CCPCC, Northwest Bureau, <u>Political-Military Problems</u> (<u>Cheng-chün wen-t'i</u> 政軍問題), May 1943, 290.807/447/3852; Jen Pi-shih, "Opinions on Several Problems" ("Kuan-yü chi-ko wen-t'i ti i-chien" 關於幾個問題的意見), <u>Dawn</u>, 1:1, April 1943, pp. 1-44.

12. T'an Cheng (譚政), <u>Military and Government and Intra-Unit Political Work Problems</u> (<u>Chün-cheng chün-tui cheng-chih kung-tso wen-t'i</u> 軍政軍隊政治工作問題), Huai-nan Military District, 1945, no BIC number.

13. Shansi-Chahar-Hopeh Military District, Political Department, <u>Directive on Production and Mass Movement Work</u> (<u>Sheng-ch'an min-yun kung-tso ti chih-shih</u> 生產民運工作的指示), May 1944, #16, 594.839/740/4428; <u>On Officer-Soldier Relationships</u> (<u>Kuan-yü kuan-ping kuan-hsi</u> 關於官兵關係), Chi-Lu-Yü Daily Press, editors, May 1945, 590.86/732/4169; Ministry of Defense, Information Office, <u>The Chinese Communists on Military Civilian Relationships</u> (<u>Chung-kung lun chün-min kuan-hsi</u> 中共論軍民關係), Chungking, 1945, 590.86/811/10197. This is a reprint by the Nationalist Government of a Chinese Communist publication on the "Cherish the People, Protect the Government" Movement (1943-1945) which was initiated in the Chin-Sui Military district in 1942 and expanded throughout the entire military in 1943.

14. A sampling of authors would include Ch'en I, Hsiao Hsiang-jung, Shu T'ung, Wang Shou-t'ao, Liu Po-ch'eng, Wang Chen, Lu Cheng-ts'ao, T'an Cheng, Wang Chia-hsiang, Kuo Hua-jo, Tso Chuan, Li Kuo-hua, Yang Ch'eng-wu, P'eng Hsueh-feng, and Huang Yung-sheng.

15. Central Investigation and Statistical Office, <u>General Situation of the New Fourth Army</u> (Hsin-ssu-chün kai-k'uang t'i-yao 新四軍概況提要), no date, 590.8/815/4746; <u>The Organization and Utilization of the Chinese Communist Army</u> (Chung-kung chih chün-tui tsu-chih yü yun-yung 中共之軍隊組織與運用), Chungking, 1942, 590.8/842/8846.

16. <u>Personal Relations and Factional Struggle Among the Communist Bandits</u> (Kung-fei nei-pu jen-shih kuan-hsi chi p'ai-hsi tou-cheng 共匪內部人事關係及派系鬥爭), in Research Group on Communist Military Affairs (Tui kung chün-shih yen-chiu-hui 對共軍事研究會), <u>Collection on Communist Bandit Military Affairs</u> (Kung-fei chün-shih ts'ung-shu 共匪軍事叢書), Taipei, 1953, 590.808/814/22716.

17. Kunming Military Region, Political Department, <u>National Defense Fighters</u> (Kuo-fang chan-shih 國防戰士), 1972, no BIC number.

12. Central Investigation and Statistical Bureau, General Office of the New Fourth Army, 新四军军部总调查统计局 and 敌

    调查統計局与 Circulation and Utilization of Communist Currency, 共产党货币的流通与利用, China Quarterly, 中国季刊,

    没有季刊 期刊 文章 文章, 新四军货币, 中国季刊, 文章, revolving, revolving

13. Taiwan's Resistance and Patriotic Struggle Against the Communist Bandits (Report on the armed anti-Communist struggle), 台湾反抗 爱国 反共 斗争 斗争 的 报告, Research Group on Communist Affairs, 共党研究, China Mainland 中国大陆 期刊 文章 文章 文章, 共产, Communist Bandit Military Affairs, 共匪军事, 中国大陆, revolving 共军 文章 文章 文章, 共产党研究, 中国大陆, revolving revolving revolving

14. Work-Study Military Report, Political Department, National Defense Ministry, 国防部 总政治部 工作 工 (二十), 1972, no. 20, 文章 number.

V. RESISTANCE BASE AREAS

When the Eighth Route Army arrived at the Wu-t'ai Mountains
in East Shansi in September 1937, political workers began mobilizing
peasants and reorganizing the local government to create a guerrilla
base. By early January 1938, the Communists had founded a resistance base area along the Shansi-Hopeh border, known as the Chin-
Ch'a-Chi Border Region. It was one of over nineteen Communist
areas created in the war and scattered behind Japanese lines from
Jehol in the north to Hainan Island in the south. The existing research by scholars on the War of Resistance has centered on Mao
Tse-tung's base of operations in Yenan and the Shen-Kan-Ning Border
Region. The BIC has extensive materials on many of the other resistance bases, particularly the Huai-pei, and Chi-Lu-Yü Border Regions.[1]
The sources fall into three broad categories--government and administrative orders, government gazettes, and materials on economic construction.

In its intelligence gathering, the Bureau collected a variety of
administrative documents from the many border area governments.
For the most part the information is incomplete, providing only a few
pieces to the jigsaw puzzle of local politics. Although these documents
are scattered and few in numbers they cover a number of interesting
topics such as transportation problems,[2] information on government and
military supply,[3] export-import regulations,[4] and border area conference reports.[5] A more informative source is the accounts of the creation and development of specific base areas.[6] The archive has a
large number of these, such as a 400-page report of early mobilization
activities in the region that eventually became the Chin-Sui Border Region.[7]

As a supplement to Communist materials, the BIC has a large
number of intelligence reports compiled by the Bureau's own agents
in the base areas. Typically, these are detailed studies of personnel
and policies, which include leadership lists extending from the border
area executive committee to the county magistrate level.[8] A comparison with Japanese intelligence reports and Communist statements from
after 1949 on the war in such collections as the Red Flag Waves
(Hung-ch'i p'iao-p'iao) shows that Nationalist information on personnel
in the border area--at least as to the identities of office holders--was

highly accurate.   Biographical information is interesting but frequently lacks credibility.

A second major source on the base areas is the Bureau's collection of various government gazettes and newspapers from the period. Although incomplete, the Bureau does have government gazettes from a number of bases including Chin-Ch'a-Chi, Central Hopeh, Chi-Lu-Yü, Huai-pei and Shantung. [9]   There are a number of base area newspapers such as the New Fourth Army's Resistance (K'ang-ti pao) and the Chin-Ch'a-Chi Military District's Resistance Weekly (K'ang-ti chou-pao), but because newspapers are not catalogued it is impossible to make a knowledgeable appraisal of these holdings.   A researcher must have some prior knowledge of the names of the principal newspapers from a specific region in order to request this type of material. [10]

The BIC has important holdings of two major Communist newspapers of this period.   First, with the exception of volume six, the Bureau has a nearly complete set of the Masses (Ch'ün-chung) for the war years. [11]   This paper was edited by P'an Tzu-nien and was the major Communist weekly in the Nationalist wartime capitals of Hankow and Chungking.   Second, Liberation (Chieh-fang) was the Communists' weekly in their own capital at Yenan from 1937 to 1941.   (The microfilm of Liberation available in the United States lacks thirty-four issues; twenty-one of these issues are in the Bureau. [12])

The BIC's richest sources on the resistance base areas deal with the economy, particularly the Great Production Drive (1943-1946).   This mass movement to increase production stressed collectives, mutual aid, household planning, model heroes, and military participation in production.   A good source on mutual labor in the BIC is a 300-page collection of essays edited by Chang Ching-fu on the development, organization, and use of the various mutual labor forms in Shen-Kan-Ning. [13] Another 300-page volume edited by the Chin-Sui Party Bureau includes all the major pronouncements on the economy by Mao Tse-tung and Kao Kang, the resolutions of the various economic conferences of the period, summations of experiences during the Great Production Drive in the two border regions, and sections on cooperatives and draft animals. [14]   There are also a number of smaller studies on local economic situations in Shen-Kan-Ning and Chin-Sui.   Yang Ssu-i, for example, wrote a detailed account on family and community economic planning, [15] and the Chin-Sui Administrative Office issued a report on that region's mutual aid problems. [16]   In addition, materials are available on the

economy from other border regions, such as Central Hopeh, the T'ai-
yueh District, Central Kiangsu, Shantung, and the Honan-Hopeh regions.[17] In this same genre, the BIC has an interesting and detailed
study from the Chi-Lu-Yü area on one local community's experience
with cooperatives and mutual labor.[18] The author incorporated a
number of statistical surveys and tables into the study and provided
concrete examples of local experiences. A researcher in this area
should also check the Bureau of Intelligence Library for local studies
from Shantung and Chi-Lu-Yü.

For the economic historian there are a number of more specialized studies on specific aspects of the economy from all of the various
base areas. Among them are accounts of the textile industry in Shen-
Kan-Ning;[19] and a number of case studies on cooperative management
and organization, such as a detailed analysis of the Nan-ch'ü Cooperative in Shen-Kan-Ning, which was perhaps the Communists' most suc-
cessful operation in cooperative work.[20] There is also a discussion
of medicine cooperatives in Central Hopeh,[21] particularly in An-kuo,
Hopeh, which prior to the war had been a center for medicine trade
for the whole nation with a tradition dating back over 1000 years.

The BIC has also some documents on banking, marketing, and
finance in the base areas, which are not plentiful, but include some
accounts of value and considerable length. For example, there are
two descriptions of credit and banking activities in the Chin-Chi-Lu-
Yü area from the T'ai-hang District Bank.[22] The Bureau also has a
publication of the Central China Military District which discusses trade,
banking practices, and the regulation of currency.[23] A number of these
documents on finance are work directives, regulations, or circulars
issued by specific economic or trade agencies.[24] The BIC also has
an occasional government plan on financial and economic work.[25]

The material in the Bureau archives on the economy generally
reflects the diversity of local experiences and independence in operations that were a part of the wartime economic development program.
At the same time, although the Communists allowed a wide margin for
local initiative in this area, documents in the BIC provide material for
a thorough study of the leadership's thinking on this subject before the
Soviet model for modernization was adopted in the early 1950s.

FOOTNOTES TO CHAPTER V

1. After 1939, the Chinese Communists effectively eliminated Nationalist military forces and their intelligence operations from North China. Not until the Civil War began in 1946 did Nationalist agents reenter these regions, and then only Shantung was thoroughly penetrated. In Central China, however, particularly in the Kiangsu-Anhwei region, there was an extensive intelligence operation under the command of Major General Tai Li (戴笠), who was the Deputy Chief and de facto head of the Military Investigation and Statistical Office until his death in 1946. Many BIC documents from this region are marked with the chop of a single intelligence office. Shen-Kan-Ning and, more particularly, Yenan, appear to have been open to Nationalist intelligence agents up to 1942-1943. Thereafter, materials in the BIC from these regions drastically decrease, reflecting the success of the Rectification Drive's cadre screening program in ferreting out Nationalist agents.

2. Chi-Lu-Yü, Administrative Office, Decisions and Orders of the Communications Conference (Chiao-t'ung hui-i chueh-ting ming-ling 交通會議決定命令), 1945, 575.29/720/ 12038.

3. Chi-Lu-Yü, Administrative Office, The Supply System of Chi-Lu-Yü in 1946 for the Government and Civilians (Chi-Lu-Yü san-shih-wu-nien-tu cheng-min kung-chi chih-tu 冀魯豫三 十五年度政民供給制度), 1946, 575.29/726/ 7094.

4. Chi-Lu-Yü, Eleventh District Office, Order Prohibiting Local Cloth and Thread for Export (Yen chin t'u-pu t'u-hsien ch'u-pu ling 嚴禁土布土線出埠令), 1945, 575.29/726/ 12807.

5. Chi-Lu-Yü, Administrative Office, Chairman Hsu's Summary Report at the Administrative Officers' Conference (Hsu chu-jen tsai chuan-yuan lien-hsi-hui shang ti tsung-chieh pao-kao 徐 主任在專員聯席會上的總結報告), 1945, 575.2907/726/7105.

6. The Northwest Shantung Anti-Japanese Base Area (K'ang-Jih ken-
    chü-ti Lu-hsi-pei-ch'ü 抗日根據地魯西北區),
    1939, 575.29/231/7171; Chi-Lu-Yü Border Region, Second Middle
    School, editor, The Establishment of a Base Area (Ken-chü-ti ti
    chien-she 根據地的建設), no date, 575.2917/876.

7. Second War Zone, General Mobilization Committee, War Zone
    General Mobilization (Chan-ti tsung tung-yuan 戰地總
    動員), 1939, 2nd of two volumes, 592.92/816/7132.

8. Central Investigation and Statistical Office, General Situation of
    the Chi-Lu-Yü Border Region (Chi-Lu-Yü pien-ch'ü kai-k'uang
    冀魯豫邊區概況), 1939, 575.29/815/7066; Cen-
    tral Investigation and Statistical Office, Intelligence Report on
    Communist Activities in North China (Hua-pei kung-tang huo-tung
    ch'ing-pao 華北共黨活動情報), handcopied, 1939,
    270.11/815/13030.

9. Chin-Ch'a-Chi Border Region, Administrative Committee, Border
    Government Gazette (Pien-cheng tao-pao 邊政導報),
    weekly, 1939-1947, 1:34-56, 3:3, 4, 28, 4:7, 8, 7:4, 5, 052.2/
    720 and 573.08/810; Central Hopeh, Administrative Office, Central
    Hopeh Gazette (Chi-chung tao-pao 冀中導報), 1946-1947,
    #771, 776, 909-911, 1453, no BIC number; Chin-Chi-Lu-Yü Bor-
    der Region, Administrative Committee, Border Area Government
    Report (Pien-ch'ü cheng-pao 邊區政報), #13-15, 17, 53-55,
    63, 64, 052.1/720; Chi-Lu-Yü, Administrative Committee, Sec-
    retariat, Chi-Lu-Yü Government Report (Chi-Lu-Yü cheng-pao
    冀魯豫政報), 1943, 575.29/726; Huai-pei Administrative
    Office, Secretariat, Government Work Bulletin (Cheng-fu kung-tso
    t'ung-hsun 政府工作通訊), 052.2/721; Shantung Admin-
    istrative Office, Democracy Gazette (Min-chu tao-pao 民主
    導報), 575.29/ 723.

10. New Fourth Army, Political Department, Resistance (K'ang-ti
    pao 抗敵報), 1939-1940, no BIC number; Chin-Ch'a-Chi
    Military District, Resistance Weekly (K'ang-ti chou-pao 抗
    敵週報), 1:4, 7, 9, 13, 14, 21, 24, 2:1, 2, 21, 22, 3:1,
    2; 052.4/8076; a useful list of Communist newspapers from the
    War of Resistance is available in Wang Ta-chung (王大中),
    *A Critical Examination of Chinese Communist Party Propaganda
    Work (Chung-kuo kung-ch'an-tang hsuan-ch'uan kung-tso tsung

chien-t'ao 中國共產黨宣傳工作總檢討),
Victory Press, 1941, available at the Hoover Library.

11. Masses (Ch'ün-chung 群眾), Hankow, 1937-1938, Chungking,
1938-1946, and Shanghai, 1946-1949, 1:3, 4, 6-8, 12, 13, 15,
18-25; 2:1-25; 3:1-25; 4:1-18; 5:1-14; 6:1-12; 7:1-4, 7-12, 14-
23; 8:1-24; 9:1-24, 052.19/813. Hoover has only scattered
issues in Volumes 1 through 9.

12. Liberation (Chieh-fang 解放), Yenan, 1937-1941; the issues
found in the BIC include numbers 24-26, 62, 65, 104, 108-112,
115, and 118-126. Many of these are in bad condition and
bookworms have caused extensive damage. However, Liberation,
has survived much better than Liberation Daily, which has been
mutilated by researchers as well as eaten by insects.

13. Chang Ching-fu (張勁夫), Mutual Labor in the Border Regions (Pien-ch'ü ti lao-tung hu-chu 邊區的勞動互助),
no date, 554.18/369/6743.

14. *CCPCC, Chin-Sui Bureau, Get Organized! Documents of the
Shen-Kan-Ning and Chin-Sui Border Regions Concerning the Production Movement (Tsu-chih ch'i-lai! Shan-Kan-Ning Chin-Sui
pien-ch'ü kuan-yü sheng-ch'an yun-tung ti wen-chien 組織
起來! 陝甘寧晉綏邊區關於生產運動
的文件), 1944, 553.59/43/6767.

15. Yang Ssu-i (楊思毅), An Introduction to Village Work Experiences (Hsia-hsiang kung-tso ching-yen chieh-shao 下鄉
工作經驗介紹), 1943, 553.59/470/6894.

16. Chin-Sui Border Region, Administrative Committee, Several
Concrete Problems of Mutual Labor (Pien-kung hu-chu ti chi-ko
chu-t'i wen-t'i 變工互助的幾個具體問題),
no date, 554.18/810/6958.

Pien-kung was a traditional form of mutual labor indigenous to
North Shensi and one of several cooperative labor forms encouraged by the Communists in North China during the Great Production Drive (1943-1946). Others included, in Central Hopeh,
pao-kung (包工), and in Central and Western Hopeh, po-kung
(撥工). Pien-kung related only to exchanges of technical

assistance for manual labor; pao-kung involved labor pools in secret society arrangements and was highly commercialized; and, po-kung, the most comprehensive of the three forms, included the sharing of labor, tools, and draft animals among several households.

17. Central Hopeh Gazette Office, Production Experiences and Production Tasks (Sheng-ch'an ching-yen yü sheng-ch'an jen-wu 生產經驗與生產任務), 1946, 553.59/816/6904; T'ai-yueh Military District, Political Department, Collection on Production Experiences (Sheng-ch'an ching-yen hui-chi 生產經驗彙集), 1945, 553.59/734/7997; Unite Labor Strength with Military Might (Lao-li yü wu-li chieh-ho ch'i-lai 勞力與武力結合起來), Central Kiangsu Press, 1945, 553.59/850/6824; Honan-Hopeh Border Region, Directives on Winter Plowing (Kuan-yü tung-keng ti chih-shih 關於冬耕的指示), 1943, 554.18/726/6844; Central Shantung Government Office, Introduction to Mutual Labor Experiences (Pien-kung hu-chu ching-yen chieh-shao 變工互助經驗介紹), 1946, New China Bookstore, 554.1807/725/6773.

18. Li Ch'un-lan (李春蘭), Shining Examples of Cooperatives and Mutual Labor Production (Ho-tso hu-chu sheng-ch'an ti huo yang-tzu 合作互助生產的活樣子), Chi-Lu-Yü Bookstore, no date, 553.59/144/6854.

19. Lung-tung District Committee (隴東地委), Investigation of the Textile Industry in Hsi-hua-chih and Pan-ma-chih (Hsi-hua-ch'ih Pan-ma-ch'ih ch'eng fang-chih tiao-ch'a 西華池盤馬赤城紡織調查), 1944, 555.282/820/6907.

20. Northwest Bureau, Research Office, The Organization, Transit, and Cooperative Experiences of the Southern District Cooperative (Nan-ch'ü ho-tso-she tsu-chih yun-shu ho-tso ti ching-yen 南區合作社組織運輸合作的經驗), 1944, 559.8/806/7995.

21. Central Hopeh Committee, Decision on the Development of the Past Year's Cooperative Enterprises in Central Hopeh, and Present and Future Work (Chi-chung i-nien lai ho-tso shih-yeh ti fa-chan chi chin-hou kung-tso chueh-ting 冀中一年來合作

事業的發展及今後工作決定),
June 1946, 539.8/726/7996.

22. South Hopeh Bank and T'ai-hang Bank, <u>Materials on Credit Work
Models</u> (Hsin-huo kung-tso tien-hsing ts'ai-liao 信貸工
作典型材料), 1947, 559.35/884/8023; Tai-hang Bank,
Work Reference Materials Committee, <u>Reference Materials on
Bank, Labor, and Commerce Work</u> (Yin-hang kung shang kung-
tso ts'an-k'ao tzu-liao 銀行工商工作參考資料),
1945, 562.82/814/7910.

23. Central China Military District, <u>Trade and Currency Work</u> (Mao-
i chin-jung kung-tso 貿易金融工作), 1945, 501.18/
742/7866.

24. Lung-tung Administrative Office, <u>Directives on Finance Work</u>
(Ts'ai-cheng kung-tso ti chih-shih hsin 財政工作的指
示信), 1942, 566.8/730/8020; Border Region Trade Management Office, <u>Collection of the Kiangsu-Anhwei Border Region
Trade Management Regulations</u> (Su-Wan pien-ch'ü huo-kuan fa-
kuei hui-pien 蘇皖邊區貨管法規彙編), 1945,
558.192/811/7906; Shen-Kan-Ning Border Region, Trade Company,
<u>Work Procedures of the Shen-Kan-Ning Border Region Trade Com-
pany</u> (Shan-Kan-Ning pien-ch'ü mao-i kung-ssu yeh-wu hsu-chih
陝甘寧邊區貿易公司業務須知),
1944, 558.2956/812/7889; Chin-Chi-Lu-Yü Border Region, <u>Direc-
tives on Finance Work</u> (Ts'ai-cheng kung-tso ti chih-shih hsin
財政工作的指示信), 1945, 15 items, 566.8/810.

25. Chin-Ch'a-Chi Bureau, <u>The Direction of Finance and Economic
Work</u> (Ts'ai-cheng ching-chi kung-tso fang-chen 財政經
濟工作方針), 1946, 566.807/720/8025.

VI. BIOGRAPHIES

Also to be noted in the Bureau archives are many biographies and commemorative volumes on Communist leaders, model workers, and heroes. They offer anecdotes and details of the everyday life of Communist cadres and, more generally, of Chinese people in the revolutionary upheavals since the 1920s. For example, there are a number of accounts of model production heroes from the Great Production Drive (1943-1946).[1] One of the most informative sources is an eleven-volume series published by the Northwest Bureau on the work of model heroes in Shen-Kan-Ning.[2] It includes the biographies of all of the major production heroes and provides good examples of the standards that the Communist Party sought in its production work. There are also several books and statements by former Communists in the BIC with intimate, if biased, accounts of the Communist movement.

In addition, documents dispersed throughout the collection offer information for political biographies of leading figures in the CCP. These include P'eng Teh-huai and Liu Po-ch'eng from the Army; Party leaders such as Ch'in Pang-hsien and P'eng Chen; activists in the women's movement like Chang Ch'in-ch'iu and Meng Ch'ing-shu; the Communist Youth League organizer Li Ch'ang; participants in the literary movement, such as Ting Ling; plus Communist intellectuals such as Ai Ssu-ch'i[3] and Fan Wen-lan. Scholars can also trace the association of certain prominent Communists with the evolution of particular themes in Chinese Communist ideology. There is sufficient material, for example, to analyze Ch'en Po-ta's evolving views on traditional Chinese philosophy in the late 1930s.[4]

FOOTNOTES TO BIOGRAPHIES

1. Chin-Sui Border Region, Administrative Office, <u>A Collection of Important Documents from the Fourth Conference on Model Heroes</u> (Ti-ssu tz'u ch'ün-ying ta-hui chung-yao wen-hsien chi 第四次群英大會重要文獻集), 1944, 575.29/720/7110.

2. Northwest Bureau, Propaganda Bureau, <u>Model Party Member and Laborer, Comrade Shen Chang-lin</u> (Mo-fan tang-yuan ho lao-tung ying-hsiung Shen Chang-lin t'ung-chih 模範黨員和勞動英雄申長林同志), 1944, 299.32/806/6782. All eleven in the series are under the call number 299.32/806.

3. Ai Ssu-ch'i (艾思奇) et. al., <u>On Attitudes Toward Study</u> (Lun hsueh-hsi ti t'ai-tu 論學習的態度), 1947, 244/108/0031-1684.

4. See, Ch'en Po-ta, "The Origins of China's Ancient Philosophy," ("Chung-kuo ku-tai che-hsueh fa-tuan" 中國古代哲學發端), <u>Liberation</u>, #62, January 1939; and, "The Philosophy and Thought of Mo Ti," ("Mo-tzu che-hsueh ssu-hsiang 墨子哲學思想), <u>Liberation</u>, #104, April 1940, and #102, March 1940.

VII. CONCLUSION

The archives of the Bureau of Investigation offer rich source material on the Chinese Communist movement from 1927 to 1953. Indeed, the major attraction of the BIC is its great variety of documents, which reflects the diversity of ideas and practices in the CCP and suggests new approaches to scholarship. In this conclusion, we will discuss some of the potential contributions of research in the BIC to the fields of political science and history.

First, many of the documents cited above provide substantial data relevant to important questions previously addressed in studies of the Chinese Communist movement For instance, Jean Chesneaux in The Chinese Labor Movement, 1919-1927 explored the causes of the collapse of the communist-led labor movement during the period of the First United Front.[1] He concluded that it lay primarily in the failure of "political strategy," particularly the "appeasement policy" of the CCP in its alliance with the Kuomintang.[2] However, data available in the BIC, such as the reports issued after April 1927 by the All-China General Labor Union on grass-roots labor organization, indicate that the failure was also of a more fundamental, organizational character. Although the Chinese Communists were supporters of European and Soviet-styled industrial unions, which were highly centralized to maximize the political influence of the proletariat, in reality, many of the CCP-affiliated unions in the late 1920s were fragmented along regional (t'ung-hsiang) lines and still dominated by patron-client relationships characteristic of the traditional labor pang and guilds.[3] In short, the destruction of the communist labor movement was also a function of the inability of the CCP leadership to overcome "feudal" influences among the working class as a basis for creating radical new forms of labor organization. Though this argument does not necessarily contradict Chesneaux's thesis, it demonstrates that research, based on secret materials from the grass-roots level, as opposed to Chesneaux's almost exclusive reliance on published documents issued by Party elites, provides a different perspective on the roots of the communists' failure to build a powerful labor movement in the 1920s.

A second potential contribution of the BIC regards the on-going debate over the appeal of nationalism versus class struggle in the period of the War of Resistance. Chalmers Johnson argues that the

85

CCP harnessed the peasants' anti-Japanese sentiment as its primary basis of mass support, while Mark Selden cites the communists' appeal to programs of economic and social revolution to explain their rise to power.[4] In each case, however, the vastly different interpretations of these authors reflect the biases of their particular documentary sources. Johnson's data, drawn from Japanese intelligence reports, came from Central China in a period preceding the implementation of rent and interest reduction campaigns and provide little evidence of the use of class struggle in stimulating peasant support. On the other hand, because Selden focuses on Yenan, which had a long revolutionary tradition based on land reform and which also remained outside the war zone, his sources generally obscure the vital role of patriotism in the Chinese Communist movement. Documents in the BIC from the North China bases, particularly from consolidated areas such as the T'ai-hang District in Chin-Chi-Lu-Yü, demonstrate that as early as 1939 struggles over rent and interest reduction had played a crucial role in stimulating peasant activism and, thus, challenge Johnson's assertion there was little social-economic significance to the Chinese Communist revolution. However, these same materials also indicate the crucial importance of nationalist themes in communist ideology. Indeed, the base areas offer an ideal laboratory for understanding the relationship between the development of a people's war and the policies of the New Democracy.

Thirdly, BIC documents lend themselves to a reinterpretation of the role of particular elites in shaping the course of the Chinese Communist revolution. Materials issued in Shanghai and the Kiangsi Soviet in the early 1930s and under the authority of the Russian Returned Students, for instance, demonstrate the early contributions of this elite to basic elements of communist strategy, such as the "mass line," and internal Party rectification (cheng-feng). Conversely, the Bureau's holdings of documents from the Northern China base areas and the Eighth Route Army suggest a less Mao-centered interpretation regarding the origins of the Chinese Communist approach to a people's war. Mao emerges in these years less an innovator than a synthesizer of CCP policies and practices.

Finally, the Bureau's archives provide new perspectives on the historical antecedents of many policy disputes which have shaped the PRC since 1949. In light of the Cultural Revolution and, more particularly, the revelations contained in the document Long Live the

Thought of Mao Tse-tung (1969), it appears that important members
of the Chinese leadership adhered to a concept of economic development which was at odds with the Soviet model in ascendency during
the early 1950s.[5] On the basis of Mao's post-1949 critiques of the
Soviet model, the BIC offers valuable data from which to judge the
uniqueness of the Maoist model of economic development as it was
formulated and implemented in the resistance and civil war years.

These are only some of the many questions and areas of controversy which are important in the fields of political science and
history. Further research in the Bureau of Investigation, as well
as other libraries and archives, will begin to provide some of the
complex answers.

FOOTNOTES TO CONCLUSION

1. Jean Chesneaux, The Chinese Labor Movement, 1919-1927.

2. Ibid., p. 409.

3. This is the conclusion, for example, of the Report on Kiangsu by the All-China General Labor Union, 1929, cited above.

4. Chalmers Johnson, Peasant Nationalism and Communist Power; and Mark Selden, The Yenan Way in Revolutionary China.

5. For a discussion of this document, see Appendix B.

VIII.   APPENDICES

A.   Bureau of Intelligence, Ministry of Defense

The Research Library, Bureau of Intelligence, Ministry of Defense (國防部　情報局　), is an important reference and research library which most scholars would find convenient to use in conjunction with the Bureau of Investigation.   The library is located near Tse-shan-yen in Shih-lin, Taipei City, Taiwan, and the same procedures for admittance to the Bureau of Investigation apply to this institution.   The library has over 40,000 volumes of which 30,000 are Chinese Communist publications since 1949.   In addition there are 900 volumes in Japanese, 300 volumes in Russian, and 1800 volumes in English on International and Chinese Communism.   Many of the documents listed below are available in the United States.

The library has the largest collection of post-1949 Chinese Communist newspapers available to the researcher on the island.   They include the People's Daily (Peking: Jen-min jih-pao 人民日報 , 1951-1974), Kuang-ming Daily (Peking: Kuang-ming jih-pao 光明日報 , 1953-1959, 1961-1974), Workers Daily (Peking: Kung-jen jih-pao 工人日報 , 1953-1966), Ta-kung-pao (Hong Kong: 1949-1974; Tientsin: 1953-1959 大公報), China Youth (Peking: Chung-kuo ch'ing-nien-pao 中國青年報), Mongol News (Meng-ku hsiao-hsi pao, 1966-1968, 1970-1972, 蒙古消息報), Wen-hui-pao (Shanghai: Wen-hui-pao 文匯報 , 1956-1959), Yangtze Daily (Wuhan: Chang-chiang jih-pao 長江日報 , partial 1951-1957), South China Daily (Canton: Nan-fang jih-pao 南方日報 , 1950-1958, 1972-1974), and the Yunnan Daily (Kun-ming: Yun-nan jih-pao 雲南日報 , 1971-1973).

The library also holds a collection of 245 different Red Guard newspapers.   They are primarily from the Kwangtung region, and for most papers there are only from one to three issues.   However, there are several with longer runs, including The East is Red (Tung-fang-hung 東方紅 , 1967-1968, 15 issues), Sun Yat-sen University Red Flag (Canton: Chung-ta hung-ch'i 中大紅旗, 1968, 11 issues), New Peking University (Peking: Hsin Pei-ta 新北大 , 1967, 7 issues), Canton Peasant Union (Canton: Kuang-chou nung-tai-hui 廣州農代會 , 1970-1971, 13 issues), and the Canton Red Guard (Canton: Kuang-chou hung-tai-hui 廣州紅代會 , 1968-1970, 14 issues).

In addition to post-1949 materials, the library also has a small collection of original documents from the period before 1944. There are 1008 items, all of which are catalogued in the bibliography Communist Bandit Original Source Materials and Periodicals from the 1920s to the 1950s (Kung-fei erh-shih-nien-tai chih wu-shih-nien-tai yuan-shih wen-chien yü shu-k'an 共 匪 二十 年 代 至 五 十 年 代 原 始 文 件 與 書 刊). The library first published this bibliography in 1971 in conjunction with the Sino-American Conference on Mainland China, and conference organizers distributed it to a limited number of Western scholars attending. Despite the thirty year time span claimed in the title, the majority of the material dates from the 1940s and originates from the Shantung base area, indicating that the Nationalists probably obtained it in their military operations in that province during the civil war period, 1946-1949. The major emphasis of this material is on Party and military affairs--as it is in the library generally.

The Bureau of Intelligence Library is designed for research and is not an archive like the Bureau of Investigation, where retrieval is a comparatively difficult task. Moreover, it has a broader base of secondary and reference material, than does the Institute of International Relations.

B. Institute of International Relations

The Republic of China, Institute of International Relations (Chunghua min-kuo kuo-chi kuan-hsi yen-chiu so 中 華 民 國 國 際 關 係 研 究 所) is the largest research institution on Taiwan engaged in the collection of materials on mainland China. In addition, it is the liaison office for foreign scholars in Taiwan involved in research on Chinese Communist affairs. The Institute is located in Mucha, Taipei City, and offers assistance to scholars in gaining access to the Bureau of Intelligence Library and the Bureau of Investigation Archives.

The Institute has a collection of secondary works on international politics and the Chinese Communist movement, and a number of standard reference materials and microfilm collections, such as the Ch'en Ch'eng collection. Primary research materials held by the Institute vary in scope and accessibility. There is, for instance, a large number of Chinese Communist Local Radio Reports (Chung-kung ti-fang kuang-po) published in Chinese, which are made readily available to foreign scholars. There is also the Institute's collection of daily, weekly, and monthly reports on internal Chinese Communist affairs acquired from various intelligence organizations of the Nationalist government. These are serialized and cover matters related to the Cultural Revolution (1965-1969) and the recent campaign to criticize Confucius and Lin Piao. However, the majority of these reports are classified and are not made widely accessible to researchers.

In recent years, the Institute has issued reprints of primary documents acquired from Nationalist sources on the Mainland and in Hong Kong and Thailand, which bear upon political and military affairs in China, particularly since the end of the Cultural Revolution. These include, for instance, Long Live the Thought of Mao Tse-tung (Mao Tse-tung ssu-hsiang wan-sui) [two sets of two volumes each, 1967 and 1969], Comrade Chiang Ch'ing on Literature and Art (Chiang Ch'ing t'ung-chih lun wen-i), Reference Materials Concerning Education on Situation (Hsing-shih chiao-yü ts'an-k'ao ts'ai-liao) [issued by the Kunming Military Region and more accurately translated as Reference Materials on Current Events Education], A Record of Speeches by Lin Piao (Lin Piao yü-lu), and Directives by Chairman Mao in Regard to Educational Work (Mao chu-hsi kuan-yü chiao-yü chih kung-tso ti chih-shih). These and other documents made available by the Institute are on microfilm at the Asia Library, University of Michigan.

GLOSSARIES

A. Communist Publication Houses

Chi-Lu-Yü shu-tien	冀魯豫書店
Ch'i-ch'i pao-she	七七報社
Chieh-fang	解放
Fo-hsiao	拂曉
Ho-chung	合眾
Hsiang-tao (Sacrifice League)	嚮導
Hsin-hua	新華
Hua-pei	華北
Huang-ho (Sacrifice League)	黃河
K'ang-ti she	抗敵社
Kung-jen (post-1949)	工人
Kung-lun (Chungking)	公論
Nan-fang	南方
Sheng-huo	生活
Shih-tai (post-1949)	時代
Su-pei	蘇北
Ta-chung	大眾
T'ung-i (Nationalist)	統一

B. Names and Official Titles

Ai Ch'ing	艾青	
Ai Ssu-ch'i	艾思奇	Secretary General, CCPCC, Cultural Committee.
Chang Ch'ih-min	張赤民	
Chang Ch'in-ch'iu	張琴秋	Editor, China Women, 1939-1941.
Chang Ching-fu	張勁夫	Deputy Chief, Political Department, North Yangtze Command, New Fourth Army.
Chang Tso-hua	張佐華	
Chang Wen-t'ien	張聞天	Secretary General, CCPCC, 1937-1942.
Chang Yun-i	張雲逸	Vice-commander, New Fourth Army, 1941-1945.
Ch'en Ch'ang-hao	陳昌浩	Secretary, O-Yü-Wan Youth League.
Ch'en Man-yuan	陳漫遠	District Commander, 115th Division, Eighth Route Army, 1938-1945.
Ch'en Po-ta	陳伯達	Deputy Director, CCPCC, Propaganda Department.
Ch'en Tu-hsiu	陳獨秀	Founder, CCP
Ch'en Yun	陳雲	Director, CCPCC, Finance and Economics Department.
Ch'in Pang-hsien	秦邦憲	Head, Provisional Central Political Bureau in Shanghai, 1932-1933.
Chou Shih-ti	周世弟	Director, Political Department, 120th Regiment, Eighth Route Army, 1934.
Chou Wen	周文	Secretary General, Shen-Kan-Ning Border Region Government, 1945.

Chou Yang	周揚	Director, Education Department, Shen-Kan-Ning Border Region, 1937-1940.
Chu Jui	朱瑞	Secretary, Organization Bureau, North China Bureau, 1938.
Fan Wen-lan	范文瀾	Vice-President, Central Research Academy (Yenan), 1942.
Feng Ting	馮定	Editor, <u>Resistance Weekly</u> and Director of the Political Department of the Central China branch of Resistance University, 1941.
Fu Tso-i	傅作義	
Ho Lo	何洛	Instructor, North China Unified University, 1940.
Ho Lung	賀龍	Commander, 120th Division, Eighth Route Army, 1937-1945.
Ho Tzu-shu	何子述	
Hsiao Chün	蕭軍	
Hsiao Hua	蕭華	Political Commissar, 115th Division, Eighth Route Army, 1938-1945.
Hsin An-t'ing	辛安亭	Editor, <u>Masses</u>, 1937-1945.
Hu Feng	胡風	
Huang Ching	黃敬	Secretary, Central Hopeh Committee.
Huang Hua	黃華	Member, National Liberation Vanguards of China, 1937.
Jao Shu-shih	饒漱石	Political Commissar, New Fourth Army, 1941.
Jen Pi-shih	任弼時	Official, Party Secretariat.

K'ang K'o-ch'ing	康克清	Women's Movement Leader and wife of Chu Teh.
Kao Kang	高岡	Secretary, CCPCC, Northwest Bureau, 1942.
Li Ch'ang	李昌	Leader, National Liberation Vanguards of China, 1937-1939.
Li Fu-ch'un	李富春	Deputy Director, CCPCC, Finance and Economics Department, 1942.
Li Li-san	李立三	
Li Yu	黎玉	Vice-commander, Shantung Military District, 1941.
Li Wei-han [pseudonym Lo Mai]	李維漢 (羅邁)	Director, CCPCC, United Front Work Department, 1938.
Lin Piao	林彪	Commander, 115th Division, Eighth Route Army, 1937-1945.
Lin Po-ch'ü	林伯渠	Chairman, Shen-Kan-Ning Border Region, 1938-1945.
Liu K'ai-feng	劉瞠風	Director, Education Department, Chin-Ch'a-Chi Border Government, 1941-1945.
Liu Po-ch'eng	劉伯承	Commander, 129th Division, Eighth Route Army, 1937-1945.
Liu Shao-ch'i	劉少奇	Director, CCPCC, North China Bureau, 1935-1937.
Liu Tzu-chiu	劉子久	Secretary, Kiangsu-Anhwei Committee, 1941.
Liu Ying	劉英	Women's Movement Leader and wife of Chang Wen-t'ien.

Lo Jung-huan	羅榮桓	Commander, Shantung Military District, 1941.
Mao Tse-tung	毛澤東	
Mao Tun	茅盾	
Meng Ch'ing-shu	孟慶樹	Women's Movement Leader and wife of Wang Ming.
P'an Tzu-nien	潘梓年	Editor, Hsin-hua jih-pao, 1938-1947.
P'eng Chen	彭真	Secretary, Chin-Ch'a-Chi Party Committee, 1938-1942.
P'eng Hsueh-feng	彭雪楓	Commander, Fourth Division, New Fourth Army, 1940.
P'eng P'ai	彭湃	
Po I-po	薄一波	Commander, First Column, Dare-to-Die Corps, 1939.
Sha K'o-fu	沙可夫	Principal, Lu Hsun Academy of Arts.
Sung Shao-wen	宋劭文	Chairman, Chin-Ch'a-Chi Border Region, 1938-1945.
T'an Cheng	譚政	Director, Political Department, Shen-Kan-Ning Military District, 1944.
Teng T'o	鄧拓	Editor, Chin-Ch'a-Chi Daily, 1939-1945.
Teng Tzu-hui	鄧子恢	Deputy Director, Political Department, New Fourth Army, 1941.
T'ien Fu	田夫	
Ting Ling	丁玲	Head, Women's National Salvation Association.
Tung Ch'un-ts'ai	董純才	Official, Education Department, Shen-Kan-Ning Border Region

98

Tung Hsin	董昕	
Wang Chia-hsiang	王稼祥	Director, Political Department, Eighth Route Army, 1939.
Wang Shih-wei	王實味	
Yang Ssu-i	楊思毅	
Yang Sung	楊松	Editor, Liberation Daily, 1941.
Yao Chung-ming	姚仲明	
Yen Hsi-shan	閻錫山	Governor of Shansi.
Yuan Ching	袁靜	

C. Geographical Terms

I. Provinces

Jeho	熱 河	
Suiyuan	綏 遠	

II. Border Regions, Base Areas, Soviets, and Districts

Chi-Chin	冀 晉	Hopeh-Shansi Border Region
Chi-chung	冀 中	Central Hopeh Base Area
Chi-Lu-Yü	冀 魯 豫	Hopeh-Shantung-Honan Border Region
Chin-Ch'a-Chi	晉 察 冀	Shansi-Chahar-Hopeh Border Region
Chin-Chi-Lu-Yü	晉 冀 魯 豫	Shansi-Hopeh-Shantung-Honan Border Region
Chin-Chi-Yü	晉 冀 豫	Shansi-Hopeh-Honan Border Region
Chin-Sui	晉 綏	Shansi-Suiyuan Border Region
Hai-nan	海 南	Hainan Island Base Area
Hsiang-Kan	湘 贛	Hunan-Kiangsi Base Area
Hsiang-O-hsi	湘 鄂 西	West Hunan-Hupeh Soviet
Hsiang-O-Kan	湘 鄂 贛	Hunan-Hupeh-Kiangsi Soviet
Huai-hai	淮 海	Border Region
Huai-nan	淮 南	Border Region
Huai-pei	淮 北	Border Region
Kan-hsi-nan	贛 西 南	Southwest Kiangsi Soviet
Chiang-huai	江 淮	District

Chiang-pei	江北	Military District
Lu-Sui-T'ung	邳雕銅	3rd District, Huai-pei Border Region
O-hsi	鄂西	West Hupeh Soviet
O-Yü-Wan	鄂豫皖	Hupeh-Honan-Anhwei Soviet
Pin-hai	濱海	District, Shantung
Po-hai	渤海	District, Shantung
Shen-Kan-Ning	陝甘寧	Shensi-Kansu-Ninghsia Border Region
Su-Wan-Yü	蘇皖豫	Kiangsu-Anhwei-Honan Border Region
T'ai-hang	太行	District, Southeast Shansi
T'ai-yüeh	太岳	District, Shansi-Honan
Tung-chiang	東江	Kwangtung Base Area

III. Counties

An-kuo	安國	Hopeh
Ch'ü-yang	曲陽	Hopeh
Fu-p'ing	阜平	Hopeh
I-t'eng	嶧滕	Shantung
Kuo	崞	Shansi
Liu-an	六安	Anhwei
Ta-yeh	大冶	Hupeh
Yen-ch'uan	延川	Shensi

IV. <u>Cities</u>

Amoy	廈門	Fukien
Kalgan	張家口	Hopeh
Liao-yang	遼陽	Liaoning
Wuhu	蕪湖	Anhwei
Yenan	延安	Shensi

D. Counties*

Anhwei:
  Fu-yang 阜陽
  Ho-fei 合肥
  Liu-an 六安
  Su 宿
  T'ien-chang 天長

Chekiang:
  Yung-chia 永嘉

Fukien:
  Fu-an 福安

Hopeh:
  An-kuo 安國
  Ch'ü-yang 曲陽
  Fu-p'ing 阜平
  Hsing-t'ang 行唐
  Kao-yang 高陽
  Ku-an 固安
  Li 蠡
  Ning-ho 寧河
  P'ing-ch'uan 平泉
  P'ing-shan 平山
  Shang-i 尚義

Hunan:
  Chang-sha 長沙
  Heng-yang 衡陽

Hupeh:
  Huang-an 黃安
  Shih-shou 石首
  Ta-yeh 大冶
  T'ung-shan 通山
  Yang-hsin 陽新
  Ying-shan 英山

Kiangsi:
  Hsia-chiang 峽江
  Wan-tai 萬載

Kiangsu:
  Feng 豐
  Feng-hsing 豐興
  Huai-an 淮安
  Ssu-yang 泗陽
  T'ai 泰
  Tung-hai 東海

Kwangsi:
  Meng-shan 蒙山

Shansi:
  Fu-shan 浮山
  Hsia 夏
  Kuo 崞
  T'ai-ku 太谷

Shantung:
  Ch'i-ho 齊河
  I-t'eng 嶧滕

Shensi:
  Lung-tung 隴東
  Mi-chih 米脂
  San-pien 三邊
  Sui-te 綏德
  Yen-an 延安
  Yen-ch'uan 延川

Yunnan:
  Ho-k'ou 河口

---

*This is a list of <u>hsien</u> from which materials are available in the BIC. Given the vast collection of BIC materials from local areas of CCP activity, however, this list is not exhaustive.

E. Reproduction Techniques

Carbon Copy	複寫
Hand Copied	手抄
Lead Type	鉛印
Litho	石印
Mimeograph	油印
Wood Block	木刻

F. Miscellaneous Terms

ch'ing-suan	清算
Ch'üan-kuo tsüng-kung hui	全國總工會
Chueh-ssu-tui	決死隊
Chung-hua ch'uan-kuo wen-i-chieh k'ang-ti hsieh-hui	中華全國文藝界抗敵協會
Chung-kuo min-tsu chieh-fang hsien-feng-tui	中國民族解放先鋒隊
fan-shen	翻身
hsia-fang	下放
Hsien	縣
hsueh-hsi	學習
Hua-pei Lien-ta	華北聯大
K'ang-ta	抗大
kuo-yü	國語
mi-shu-ch'u	秘書處
min-tsu hsing-shih	民族形式
Pai Ch'i	白妻
Pai Kuei	白貴
p'o-hsieh	破鞋
Shan-hsi hsi-sheng t'ung-meng-hui	山西犧牲同盟會
T'ai-p'ing-yang lao-tung ta-hui mi-shu-ch'u	太平洋勞動大會秘書處

tsa-wen   雜文

tsai-chih kan-pu   在職幹部

yang-ko   秧歌

MICHIGAN PAPERS IN CHINESE STUDIES

No. 1. The Chinese Economy, 1912-1949, by Albert Feuerwerker.

No. 2. The Cultural Revolution: 1967 in Review, four essays by
Michel Oksenberg, Carl Riskin, Robert Scalapino, and Ezra Vogel.

No. 3. Two Studies in Chinese Literature: "One Aspect of Form
in the Arias of Yüan Opera" by Dale Johnson; and "Hsü K'o's Huang
Shan Travel Diaries" translated by Li Chi, with an introduction,
commentary, notes, and bibliography by Chun-shu Chang.

No. 4. Early Communist China: Two Studies: "The Fu-t'ien Incident" by Ronald Suleski; and "Agrarian Reform in Kwangtung, 1950-
1953" by Daniel Bays.

No. 5. The Chinese Economy, ca. 1870-1911, by Albert Feuerwerker.

No. 6. Chinese Paintings in Chinese Publications, 1956-1968: An
Annotated Bibliography and An Index to the Paintings, by E. J. Laing.

No. 7. The Treaty Ports and China's Modernization: What Went
Wrong? by Rhoads Murphey.

No. 8. Two Twelfth Century Texts on Chinese Painting, "Shan-shui
ch'un-ch'üan chi" by Han Cho, and chapters nine and ten of "Hua-chi"
by Teng Ch'un, translated by Robert J. Maeda.

No. 9. The Economy of Communist China, 1949-1969, by Chu-yuan
Cheng.

No. 10. Educated Youth and the Cultural Revolution in China by
Martin Singer.

No. 11. Premodern China: A Bibliographical Introduction, by Chun-
shu Chang.

No. 12. Two Studies on Ming History, by Charles O. Hucker.

No. 13. Nineteenth Century China: Five Imperialist Perspectives,
selected by Dilip Basu, edited with an introduction by Rhoads Murphey.

No. 14. Modern China, 1840-1972: An Introduction to Sources and Research Aids, by Andrew J. Nathan.

No. 15. Women in China: Studies in Social Change and Feminism, edited with an introduction by Marilyn B. Young.

No. 16. An Annotated Bibliography of Chinese Painting Catalogues and Related Texts, by Hin-cheung Lovell.

No. 17. China's Allocation of Fixed Capital Investment, 1952-57, by Chu-yuan Cheng.

No. 18. Health, Conflict, and the Chinese Political System, by David M. Lampton.

No. 19. Chinese and Japanese Music-Dramas, edited by J. I. Crump and William P. Malm.

No. 20. Hsin-lun (New Treatise) and Other Writings by Huan T'an (43 B.C.-28 A.D.), translated by Timoteus Pokora.

No. 21. Rebellion in Nineteenth-Century China, by Albert Feuerwerker.

No. 22. Between Two Plenums: China's Intraleadership Conflict, 1959-1962, by Ellis Joffe.

No. 23. "Proletarian Hegemony" in the Chinese Revolution and the Canton Commune of 1927, by S. Bernard Thomas.

No. 24. Chinese Communist Materials at the Bureau of Investigation Archives, Taiwan, by Peter Donovan, Carl E. Dorris, and Lawrence R. Sullivan.

Price: $3.00 (US) each
except $4.00 for special issues #6, #15, and #19
and $5.00 for special issue #20

Prepaid Orders Only

MICHIGAN ABSTRACTS OF CHINESE AND
JAPANESE WORKS ON CHINESE HISTORY

No. 1. The Ming Tribute Grain System by Hoshi Ayao, translated by Mark Elvin.

No. 2. Commerce and Society in Sung China by Shiba Yoshinobu, translated by Mark Elvin.

No. 3. Transport in Transition: The Evolution of Traditional Shipping in China, translations by Andrew Watson.

No. 4. Japanese Perspectives on China's Early Modernization: The Self-Strengthening Movement, 1860-1895 by K. H. Kim.

No. 5. The Silk Industry in Ch'ing China by Shih Min-hsiung, translated by E-tu Zen Sun.

Price: $4.00 (US) each

Prepaid Orders Only

NONSERIES PUBLICATION

Index to the "Chan-Kuo Ts'e", by Sharon Fidler and J. I. Crump. A companion volume to the Chan Kuo Ts'e translated by J. I. Crump (Oxford: Clarendon Press, 1970). $3.00

Michigan Papers and Abstracts available from:
Center for Chinese Studies
The University of Michigan
Lane Hall
Ann Arbor, Michigan 48104
USA